D0255045

Pier 21
The Gateway that Changed Canada

Trudy Duivenvoorden Mitic
J. P. LeBlanc

LANCELOT PRESS
HANTSPORT, NOVA SCOTIA

Cover design: Robert Pope
Front cover photo: Sister Kelly welcomes a group of new arrivals to
Pier 21, circa 1950s. Back cover photo: troops returning to Halifax from
WWII, circa 1945.

ISBN 0-88999-406-4
First published 1988 by Lancelot Press
Reprinted 1997 by Nimbus Publishing

Nimbus Publishing Limited
3731 Mackintosh Street
PO Box 9301, Station A
Halifax, NS B3K 5N5
(902) 455-4286

Sister Florence Kelly, the "German Sister," welcomes groups of new arrivals, circa 1950.

Courtesy - Sisters of Service

Pier 21

Acknowledgements

We gratefully acknowledge the contributions made by the following groups and individuals:

The Canada Employment and
Immigration Commission
William Marks, Director of Immigration

The Halifax Jewish Historical Society
Sara Yablon

The Halifax Port Corporation
Raymond V. Beck, Past Chairman

The Public Archives of Nova Scotia
Philip Hartling, Archivist

The Roman Catholic Archdiocese of Halifax
Sister Francis Xavier, Archivist

The Sisters of Service
Sister Hilda Lunney, Director

Finally, it is fitting to acknowledge the contribution of the original "Pier 21 Story," a 1978 document compiled by the Canada Employment and Immigration Commission. That project served as the raw material and the inspiration for the development of this book.

Trudy Duivenvoorden Mitic
J.P. LeBlanc

Dedication

This book is dedicated to the
One and One-Quarter Million Canadians
who travelled through the Pier 21 Gateway.
This is their story.

Contents

Introduction / **9**

Pier 21: The Beginning / **11**

Under the Yellow Flag — Quarantine / **37**

The Great Depression / **49**

The War Years / **59**

War Brides and Refugees / **75**

People of the Pier / **105**

The Tide of Immigrants / **129**

The Ending of an Era / **157**

Epilogue / **167**

Appendix A / **173**

Appendix B / **179**

Contributors / **183**

References / **185**

Introduction

If a building could speak, if its walls could whisper, if its starkly tiled, well-trounced floors could utter a word, then Halifax's Pier 21 would have an incredible story to tell. Hers would be a tale of intense human emotions, of unexpected courage, of gladness and grief, of beginnings and endings.

For several decades the long, low-lying, waterfront shed that is Pier 21 greeted a steady stream of ocean liners filled with prospective Canadians from every part of the world. Under the cover of its drab exterior, Pier 21 served as the stage upon which unfolded some of the most exciting chapters of 20th century Canadian history.

The players in this poignant tale of human drama were the one and one-quarter million immigrants who passed through the unpretentious portals of Pier 21, their wide and uncertain eyes eager yet hesitant to catch a first glimpse of their new homeland. In the spacious reception area they milled in tightly spun whorls, women clutching children and luggage, men with hat and precious documents in hand.

Some came to seek shelter from the ravages of war and oppression. All came in search of a better life, a new beginning, a Mother Country for future generations. They came in groups large and small, some bringing a sizeable collection of possessions, others with only the clothing on their backs.

The players, too, were the three hundred and sixty thousand Canadian military personnel who departed from Canadian soil for the battlefields of Europe. Many would never return.

But if the players were the seas of people who swept through Pier 21, then the stagehands were the dedicated individuals who worked there, greeting and directing the human tides that flowed and ebbed at its doors. Quietly, unobtrusively, they staffed the Pier's many stations. Immigration officials tirelessly examined documents, processed applications, and dispensed the coveted yellow card that saw an immigrant up the first small step of the staircase to Canadian citizenship. Physicians and nurses remained at the ready to administer medical treatment, including minor surgery, in the Pier's hospital.

The matronly volunteers of the Red Cross lovingly attended to the needs of the travel-weary youngsters, bathing them and tucking them into clean cots in the Pier nursery. And the clerical team that quietly roamed the halls of the Pier reached out to those in need of both physical and spiritual reassurance.

This, then, is the story of Pier 21. It is the story of the people who worked there and the people who passed through its gates, each on his way to his own particular destiny. Each of these new arrivals has served as a weaver at the loom that is Canada. Each has added the colours and textures of his own particular culture to the Canadian tapestry in progress. And each has ensured that Canada's social fabric would be irrevocably changed, its diverseness heightened, its horizons expanded.

Pier 21 still stands today, stoic and empty, on the windy Halifax waterfront. The hustle and bustle is over, the people are gone, the ocean liners no longer sidle gingerly along its length. But the stories remain. They strain to be told.

If only the walls could whisper.

Pier 21:
The Beginning

Red Cross workers and immigrants at Pier 21, pre-WW II.

"HOLLAND-AMERICAN STEAMSHIP **NIEUW AMSTERDAM** LANDS 51 IMMIGRANTS AT NEW SHEDS AT SOUTH TERMINALS."

So read the front page headline in the March 28, 1928, issue of *The Evening Mail.* And so began one of the most colorful chapters of 20th century Canadian history.

The **Nieuw Amsterdam** was the first vessel to be received at the newly opened Pier, a large immigration complex situated on prime waterfront property in the south end of Halifax. Over the next forty years, Pier 21 was to greet and process a steady, pulsating stream of newcomers from many parts of the world. In time it was to become known as the Gateway to Canada.

Pier 21 was undisputably one of the most modern buildings of its time. It had been erected as a replacement for Pier 2, an aging, sagging structure no longer capable of handling the heavy flow of immigrant traffic to Halifax. The newly completed Pier 21 was a two-storey building, 584 feet in length and connected by covered ramps to an annex and to the nearby railway station. The building was situated on the centre section of a 2,007-foot, rock and concrete seawall that boasted a water depth of forty feet at low tide. The Halifax harbour, which was only thirty minutes steaming distance from the open sea, contained a full ten square miles of protected water with negligible tide conditions. Even the largest ships could enter and dock with relative ease and absolute safety.

The salience of the Halifax harbour had been well known for centuries; now, with the completion of a large, modern immigration facility, Halifax was to become recognized as one of the finest ports on the eastern seaboard.

The first storey of Pier 21 was to be used entirely for the handling of freight while the upper storey would house the immigration facility. This level and the Customs Annex to which it was connected by a walkway contained a large reception area (where people could and sometimes did indulge in a game of badminton), several waiting rooms, two kitchens and cafeterias that could accommodate several hundred people, a canteen, a nursery, a hospital where minor surgery could be performed, a block of ten windowless cells, detention areas, dormitories, and a promenade overlooking the harbour.

For reasons of security, it was decreed that all of the facility's windows would be barred. The entire second level was to be out-of-bounds for unauthorized personnel.

> It was a wise precaution that the Government had thrown a protective screen around the travellers, confining them to the official attentions of this family of authorized and capable workers. The refugees would otherwise have been the natural prey of unscrupulous intruders, for they were totally ignorant of all facts about this country, geographical as well as others.[41]

A 1932 edition of *The Open Gateway*, published by the Halifax Harbour Commissioners, describes the new Pier 21 with unabashed pride and a hint of patriotism:

> To the casual passerby at the Halifax Ocean Terminals, Transit Shed 21 is simply a two storey building and has nothing in its outward appearance to show that it is different from any of the other transit sheds. It is different, however, for on the second floor of this shed is housed the Halifax branch of the Canadian Immigration Department. It is here that every immigrant who enters Canada by way of Halifax first sets foot on Canadian soil. It is here that first and perhaps lasting impressions of the new country are made, and it is safe to say that the newcomer is never

disappointed with the land which he has chosen to make his new home.

Almost the whole floor of this large shed is devoted to the Immigration Department. The many windows make it nearly as bright as out and at night it is so well lighted that one can read without difficulty in almost any part of the room. The polished floors and benches add to the appearance of light and cleanliness.

Into this well-heated, lighted, and perfectly ventilated building, the immigrants are conducted immediately on leaving the boat, and they are at once taken to the general assembly room by the immigration guards. A large Union Jack hangs on the nearest wall. This emblem probably does more than anything else to impress on them that they are in a British Country; that to many of them customs, habits and even the language is new.[56]

The exact number of Immigration staff employed at Pier 21 at any one given time is not known. It is known, however, that during the peak years upwards of ten Immigration Officers would have been on duty at once, processing the long lines of new arrivals. On occasion additional officers would be called in to help when larger than usual groups of arrivals were presented for processing. This was more apt to happen in winter when the Montreal and Quebec City ports were closed due to ice conditions in the St. Lawrence River.

As well, there were the matrons who provided support for single women and women travelling with children, up to twenty-two guards, numerous caterers and kitchen and cleaning employees, and a cluster of administrative staff.

Since the ships could arrive at any time of day or night, shifts were often long and extremely busy. Morning came early for the Immigration staff; it was not uncommon to see the twinkling of lit office windows in the pre-dawn hours as staff prepared to greet yet another day's crop of future Canadians. Often an ocean liner or two which had slipped into the harbour during the night sat serenely docked at the Pier, awaiting the moment when the procession of officials would begin up the gangplank.

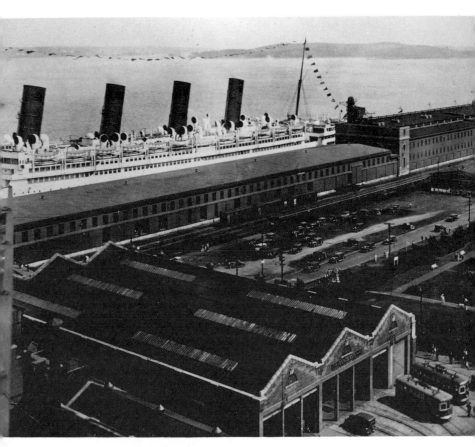

This is a composite photograph which shows a panoramic view of Piers 20, 21 and 22. (Pier 21 is the two-storey shed in the centre). The walkways/tunnels lead from Pier 21 to the Pier 21 Annex, and from the Annex to the Railway Station, located behind the

Hotel Nova Scotian. Note the tram shed in the foreground, on the left. The name of the ship on the left is unfortunately not known. 1930s or 1940s photo.

Courtesy - Halifax Port Corporation

A typical day may well have begun like this: As the darkness of night slowly lifts, often to reveal a thick grey blanket of misty fog, port workers arrive to take up their stations. Cafeteria personnel, neatly attired in white, begin the formidable task of preparing breakfast for several hundred people. Many who dine here on this particular morning will experience their first taste of Canadian cuisine.

Soon the smell of freshly brewed coffee wafts through the hallways, and the large clocks on the walls indicate that it is nearly seven a.m. A guard arrives with the manifest, the ship's passenger list, which is scrutinized by several officials and volunteers. All seems in order. The traditional parade of government officials, always led by a physician, proceeds up the gangplank. Passenger unloading does not begin until the ship has been medically cleared. Until such time, guards are placed at the gangplanks to ensure that only authorized individuals board and leave the ship.

Passengers disembarking from the ships are required to wait on the dock until their heavy baggage has been unloaded and inspected. From there they wend their way into the Pier's reception area where they are sorted into identifiable groups: families, women and children, and single men. At one end of the large room stands a series of foreboding wire cages that stretch from floor to ceiling. The immigrants are required to leave their hand baggage in the cages until they have been examined by health and immigration officials. While they wait on the benches in the reception hall, their baggage sits in the cages under lock and key.

The cages are intended solely to speed up the immigration process. Yet, in those who have endured an arduous trek across continental Europe, those who have left behind autocratic homelands for an uncertain future in an alien land, the sight of these wire confinements must instill a grave apprehension. The cages seem a blatant contradiction to all that these new arrivals have gleaned about Canada. As they spill into Pier 21 and are greeted by a wall of wire mesh, they must wonder if their insatiable quest for freedom has not unwittingly brought them full circle.

The reception area seems filled with cacophonous confusion. The staff try to maintain some semblance of order and at times their efforts appear to be in vain. Everywhere people are talking and gesticulating wildly.

The arrival of our 'New Canadians' is a scene filled with human pathos. As soon as the liner has docked and the huge hawsers have tied her to the shore the gangway is lowered. There comes filing down a pageant of all nations: the stolid British, their features hardened by the long protracted economic struggle in the old land; the Irish and Scotch with a merry twinkle in their eye; the blonde Norwegians, bewildered, yet determined; the Poles, the Ukrainians, the Russians, with their dreamy eyes and Oriental features; the Germans, systematic in all their movements; the Italians, vivacious and sentimental, smiling through their tears . . . they all come facing an enigmatic future in this land of their choice and adoption.[54]

If the boat carries immigrants of many nationalities, a common occurrence, volunteer translators have to be roused from their beds and homes, and summoned to the Pier. One translator of extraordinary capability was the Roman Catholic Port Chaplain of the time, Father Pius. Born in Kiev of Russian nobility and educated in Germany and Italy, Father Pius had impressive command of twelve formal languages and several dialects.

Following the initial examinations, the arrivals are placed into one of two categories: those to be temporarily detained because of incomplete information and documentation, illness, or lack of funds (included in this category are those who will eventually be deported), and those to be issued the status of Landed Immigrant. The arrivals to be detained are escorted to the dormitories where they will be housed until their situation can be clarified.

Within the confines of Pier 21, the detainees are well fed and well treated. Families are kept together and housed in special family quarters. Detainees can enjoy the use of a recreation room, kitchen and dining room, and a promenade overlooking the harbour. True to the tradition of the time, separate male and female quarters are maintained for British subjects and for all others, who are designated as Foreigners.

Immigration staff at Pier 21, circa 1935.

Courtesy - CEIC

The few who arouse serious doubts about their character are placed into the cells in the detention area where they will be guarded on a 24-hour basis. They can exercise on an enclosed balcony that overlooks George's Island.

The vast majority of the arrivals journey through the Pier's complex but once, their footsteps on tiled floors echoing their hopes and aspirations in the new world. They receive their Landed Immigrant status within hours of their arrival and are then allowed to proceed to the connecting ramp between the Pier and the Annex, where their hand luggage is inspected by Customs officials. This area also contains a small room where personal searches are conducted when these are deemed necessary.

Once on the mezzanine level of the Annex, the immigrants are free to purchase meals at the cafeteria and food supplies at the canteen to bolster them for the long journey inland. At a CNR wicket, they are able to purchase train tickets or verify perviously made arrangements. They then proceed through the annex and down to the heavy baggage area to claim their luggage which has in the meantime found its way, via truck, from the dock. Coopers are available to help restrap luggage that has become undone.

Meanwhile, the army of volunteers stationed in the Annex has been preparing for the moment when the arrivals will descend upon them with needs that range all the way from a bath for a grimy youngster to spiritual support for an uneasy soul. The various benevolent groups have only hours to work with the immigrants, yet they do their utmost to meet physical and spiritual needs.

"Get your money changed here!" someone shouts repeatedly from the Currency Exchange. Here and there a tired child cries feebly, elsewhere a toddler has fallen asleep on a heap of tattered suitcases.

The Redcaps, employees of the CNR, move in to help transport the unwieldy mounds of luggage to the trains. It is difficult to imagine that by nightfall the waiting reception rooms will be empty once again. Yet, before the shift is over the last document will have been stamped, the last stomach will have been filled, and the last traveller will have been ushered aboard the train to begin the final leg of his journey.

Slowly, the hallways resume their hollow echo as tired footsteps move to complete paperwork, put away hundreds of dishes, freshen up the nursery cots, and mop the endlessly tiled floors. Another day has finally come to a close.

Most of the new Canadians were carried away from Pier 21 on special immigrant trains that sat waiting on the spur lines on either side of the Annex. In the early part of this century, these "colonist" trains contained no dining facilities and few frills. The passenger cars were equipped with coal stoves at either end that did little to ward off the chill of winter.

As the trains crept westward, soot from the coal-fired engines would have found its way into the cars and settled over everything, at first timidly and then with astute boldness. Day and night the trains would have jerked and clanged their way through cities, towns, and miles of wilderness, whistling at every railway crossing. It is easy to imagine that the topic of weary conversation might have centred around the challenge of sleeping in a vibrating bed of coal dust while surrounded by harsh, obtrusive noise.

When groups of immigrants were too small to fill an entire colonist train, they were accommodated on the regular passenger trains departing from the nearby CNR railway station. These passengers found their way from the Annex to the train station by way of an overhead passageway connecting the two buildings.

Fenton C. Crosman was one of the Immigration Officers who worked at Pier 21 during the 1930s. Fascinated by the history that he saw unfolding before him on a daily basis, he kept a daily journal to serve as a perpetual witness to the uniqueness of the era. Two of his entries follow:

"HALIFAX — 25 JANUARY 1937.
. . . The Cunard **Ascania** did not dock until 5 p.m. and we were held at the office until long after seven, holding a Board on a little Welshman brought back to Canada under police auspices to face a charge of theft. He was half intoxicated and very saucy. "I'm not answering that question!" — "You fellows and hell's bells can't keep me out of Canada!" — and in milder tones, "Say, how about a cigarette?"

HALIFAX — 24 MARCH 1937.
Due to illness she had on arrival, last Friday, a
little Polish girl, age five died in our Immigration
Hospital and was buried here to-day. She was
accompanying her parents on their way to Western
Canada. The poor souls are extremely sorrowful over
this misfortune. We learn that for their benefit, Father
Pius, the Roman Catholic Immigration Chaplain,
conducted the service in the Polish language."[21]

Alison Smith was a twenty-year-old woman when she
began working at Pier 21 in 1937 as secretary to the Officer-in-
Charge, H.M. Grant. She recalls that a work week was rarely
limited to five days, often spilling over into evenings and
weekends. Still, she enjoyed the work immensely, as did most
of the staff. "It was interesting," she remembers with
enthusiasm. "You felt as if you were doing something
worthwhile." Smiling, she recalls that on many a day her boss
would warn her that things were going to get "busy, busy,
busy!" And indeed, Alison Smith spent most of her days
running around with pen and clipboard in hand, taking notes,
delivering messages, carrying out a variety of instructions, and
generally logging many miles on her well-worn shoes.

There was also a fine network of volunteers at Pier 21
that complemented the work of the Immigration and Customs
staff. Exactly when the various volunteer organizations first
began appearing on the waterfront is not known; however, the
Halifax volunteer tradition of welcoming immigrants has
roots that are steeped in the very history of the city. In 1768 a
group of Scottish settlers formed the North British Society to
provide assistance to new arrivals. The expressed purpose of
the Society was for "assisting fellow countryfolk; to facilitate
communications with other North American colonies; to
maintain kinship among Scots as well as to nurture
patriotism."[16]

The 1868 arrival of the immigrant ship, **DR Kane**,
brought a resolution "to tender the immigrants a hearty
welcome to Nova Scotia and offer them any assistance or
advice they may require."[16]

In the 1920s, Miss A.S.M. Bullock was Principal Officer of the Womens Division (Immigration). She is shown here with one of her officers.

Courtesy - CEIC

In 1919 the Canadian Council of Immigration Women was organized, with the objective to assist immigrant women. The Council established hostels at various ports of entry including Halifax. The Halifax hostel, which was located near the waterfront on Young Street, provided immigrant women and families with clean, affordable accommodation during their brief stopover in this city.

By the turn of the twentieth century, volunteer groups representing the major Christian churches as well as the Halifax Jewish community were firmly in place on the waterfront. It was recorded in 1931 that all religious representatives were housed in a single room measuring twenty by thirty feet, in the Pier's Customs Annex. This included Salvation Army personnel and chaplains from the Anglican and Roman Catholic denominations. A third chaplain represented the Presbyterian, Methodist and Baptist churches. The room also housed a Travellers' Aid counter which was staffed by an employee of the YWCA, and a booth for the Roman Catholic Sisters of Service.

The room became known as the Social Service Room and for almost forty years it witnessed a flurry of activity each time a boat full of immigrants docked in Halifax. It is in this room that volunteers heard countless tales of indescribable suffering, of hunger, of torture, and of the intense anguish that comes only from being separated from one's family. In this room the sordid details of the extremes of war were tearfully spilled out as sympathetic volunteers listened and soothed. For many immigrants who had arrived under the most trying of circumstances, this room must have marked the first step of a long journey towards the healing of the heart.

The church groups of the time were largely involved in greeting and ministering to immigrants of their own religious affiliation. Little government support was available in the 1930s; thus all of the churches attempted to provide some measure of physical and financial assistance to those immigrants who were found to be in need. As well, through the Cathlic Women's League and the Knights of Columbus, the Roman Catholic church had in place an extensive communication network that was used to inform relatives and parishes across the country of impending arrivals. This system

Jewish immigrants disembark. This is one of the last passenger loads of Jews before the restriction.

Courtesy - Halifax Jewish Historical Society

enabled many Catholic immigrants to be greeted and assisted at various points along the way to their destinations.

Halifax's small Jewish community stood ready to help the Jewish groups of arrivals who had long been recognized as being the poorest among the poor immigrants. Years before, the Canadian Jewish Congress had established the Jewish Immigrant Aid Society of Canada (JIAS), a society whose representatives in Halifax became actively involved at Pier 21. There they greeted the arrivals, often in their own languages, translated for them and bought them food and supplies whenever necessary. Frequently the members of JIAS and other local benefactors purchased train fares for those without the means to finance this final portion of their journey. Often they provided precious cash to immigrants who had arrived penniless or who were awaiting instructions and funds from relatives or sponsors living in other parts of the country.

Other Halifax-based benevolent organizations that offered assistance to an immigrant in need included the Charitable Irish, the long established North British Society and the St. George's Society. Although not many details are known about the specific projects with which each was involved, it is safe to conclude that notable contributions were made and that somewhere along the way an immigrant's spirits were uplifted and his anxieties quelled because of a caring volunteer.

Various documents highlighting the work of one particular group of volunteers reveal a legacy of selfless dedication to the needs of immigration women and children. A group of four Roman Catholic Sisters of Service arrived in Halifax in 1925, intent on providing a support system for Catholic immigrants in need. Unobtrusively, the grey-robed Sisters established a booth in the Social Service Room and, under a multilingual sign that proclaimed them to be Catholic port workers, stood ready to attend to the needs of the new arrivals. In their first year they met 177 ships with a total passenger list of 33,503 persons. Of this number, 13,000 were Roman Catholic or Greek Orthodox and representative of several nationalities.

On a daily basis, the Sisters darted in and out of the throngs of people who milled eagerly around them, providing

**Sister Mary Shostak, Sisters of Service, with new arrivals.
1920s photo.**

Photo by CLIMO, Halifax
Courtesy - Halifax Port Corporation

whatever assistance they could. They did not limit their support to spiritual needs; instead they rose to the challenge of providing a diverse range of services, as the following excerpt from a Sisters of Service report illustrates:

> As the foreign-speaking people cannot understand English or French, it is necessary to have someone speak for them in order for them to purchase food for their journey inland. The Sisters often write dozens of little food lists for these people which they present at the counter. When they receive their sack of food, it is examined and, if satisfactory, many others will borrow the slip in order to buy their food. It is the same with telegrams to their relatives advising them of their arrival.[54]

Fortuitously, the busy Sisters took time to put pen to paper, describing some of the vivid scenes that were played and replayed at Pier 21 time after countless time:

> It is intensely interesting to stroll through the immigration hall after the people have found their baggage, bought their food and have settled down for a lunch before boarding the train. Bales, bags and baskets are piled up around the pillars, their owners seated on them or near them. Over there we see a large Ukrainian family, the father seated in their midst, with a loaf of bread between his knees and a bologna under his arm. He is busily slicing off a portion of each for his hungry little ones. The mother presides over a long-necked bottle filled with water and supplies the drinks.
> ... "All aboard, All aboard." The phrase is passed on in many languages. In a few minutes every one is moving. The last few mouthfuls are hastily swallowed, baskets are shut and lids closed down. Little pots and kettles are tied onto the handles or given to the smaller children to carry; babies are rolled up and bound securely to their mothers, then the crowd presses on towards the train.[54]

The Sisters did not limit their work to greeting the new

arrivals at the waterfront. Once the last of the immigrants had been ushered onto the trains, the Sisters sat down to tackle a formidable stack of paperwork that would see each new arrival referred to the parish or diocese of his destination. The Sisters also helped many of the single women to find work, usually as domestics, and often provided them with meals and a place to stay until they had found accommodations of their own.

Like so many of the other volunteers stationed at the Pier, the Sisters stood ready to meet all ships, regardless of the hour of arrival. As well, they made regular visits to the Pier's hospital where they offered their assistance to those who were being detained there.

From the beginning, the Sisters were known for their gift of languages. According to an October 31, 1929, article in the *Halifax Evening Mail*, one of the Sisters was fluent in Slav, Polish, Hungarian and German, as well as in English. The article goes on to relate what is termed, "just an incident in the daily life of the Sisters of Service":

> She was young, very young, the dark-eyed little woman from Checko-Slovakia. It had been a long voyage and when there's not much money, one can't expect to travel first class. The boat always made her sick. Then there was Marjana — sunny-haired, blue-eyed, three-year old Marjana. If only the man who examined passengers wouldn't know she was sick! She would soon be better. Seasickness made one feel very ill, but it was not serious. There was Jan to think about — honest, hardworking Jan, who had gone ahead to this fine country, Canada, and had saved enough money to send for his Katizan and little Marjana. Suppose the man would not allow them to land — would send them back. She shuddered. As her turn approached she breathed a silent prayer. Moments of dread suspense — passed! Katizan went forward joyously, holding tight to Marjana's small hand. She was going to like this new country, she thought. If only she could understand their language — if only she could hear her native tongue!

A grey-clad, sweet-faced young Sister approached and in perfect Slav addressed herself to Katizan. Could she be of any assistance? Overjoyed, the bewildered little woman told her story: of the waiting husband out in Calgary, of the seasickness, of her dread at meeting the immigration authorities. The sweet-faced, gentle Sister was a sympathetic listener. She promised to remain with Katizan until she was safely on board the train. Was she quite sure she was strong enough for the long train journey? Katizan replied bravely — she felt better now.

All aboard! Katizan made a desperate effort to pull herself together. She must go on — Jan would be waiting. But the long voyage and the seasickness and the worry had been too much for her frail strength, and the plucky little woman collapsed.

Tenderly she was cared for. When she opened her eyes she was in a large, comfortable, spotless room and at the foot of the bed she recognized the same sweet-faced Sister who had met her at the boat. They brought her something hot. How appetizing it was and how nice it tasted. She could not remember having had anything so good in a long time. Marjana? Marjana was happy downstairs with her dolly. Yes, she might come up. Was Marjana really better?

For three days she remained there, the recipient of gentle, loving care from the Sisters of Service, she and little Marjana. Pay? They would not accept pay. She must save every cent, it was so necessary, because Jan . . . .

Now she was better. Oh, yes, she felt quite well now. She would go on. The little Sister with the gift of Languages accompanied her to the train, saw her safely on board with provision for the journey, communicated with Jan who later sent a most grateful letter of appreciation of all the Sisters had done for his Katizan and little Marjana.[55]

And so, in the brief hours between an immigrant's arrival by ship and departure by train, the Sisters worked

Red Cross workers at Pier 21 in the 1920s.
SITTING (L-R): **Miss E. Cuthbertson, Mrs. F.H. Withers, Mrs. C.W. Lutes, Miss S. O'Grady, Miss C. Powell, Mrs. P.J. McManus, Mrs. R.A. Millson, Mrs. I. Dodwell, Mrs. W.H. Bullock.**
STANDING (L-R): **Mrs. Boyd, Mrs. J. Spiro, Miss McIntosh, Miss M. Zwicker, Mrs. V.M. Schenk, Miss V. Smith, Miss Anna Lee, Mrs. Ruderfrod, Mrs. N.V. Gastonguay, Mrs. Carl Appter.**
MISSING: **Mrs. W.H. Cunningham, Miss Faulkner, Miss L. Brown.**

Photo by CLIMO, Halifax
Courtesy - Halifax Port Corporation

diligently and with complete dedication. Their presence at the Pier provided the newcomers with tangible proof that Canada was indeed a good country to come home to.

There is yet another group of volunteers whose sizeable contribution to immigration bears documentation in the annals of Pier 21 history. The International Red Cross is known throughout the world for its compassion for humankind. For years the Canadian Red Cross Society maintained a strong presence on the Halifax waterfront. Adjacent to the Social Service Room was a large, comfortable nursery that was operated by an efficient team of Red Cross volunteers. With its airy brightness, generous furniture, and twelve white cribs made up with crisp, clean linens, the nursery must have been a most welcome sight to the grime-encrusted, travel-weary families who presented themselves to the Red Cross workers.

While parents soothed their tired limbs in tubs of hot, sudsy water, the Red Cross team scrubbed the youngsters and changed them into clean clothing, issued free of charge to those in need. Infants were settled into the cribs for a nap while parents and children enjoyed a lunch provided by the Red Cross. Weary mothers could rest on one of seven cots situated near the cribs for the time that remained until the departure of the trains.

A team of up to twenty volunteers manned the nursery on an around-the-clock basis. The services of the Red Cross were available to all at no cost. Donations were, however, gratefully accepted and were used to further the services at Pier 21. During the lull between ships, linens were washed, beds were remade, and stocks were replenished. It is not difficult to imagine that this tangible, physical form of assistance must have brought great satisfaction to the volunteers and immense joy to the new arrivals. Undoubtedly, an atmosphere of cheeriness must have prevailed in the nursery as clean babies were cuddled and youngsters with freshly scrubbed, red cheeks beamed from behind their biscuits and tin cups of milk. Given this kind of genuine welcome, even the parents must have allowed their greater worries and anxieties to subside for the moment.

The people of Pier 21 were a living, moving chain of

New arrivals enjoy their first snack in a new land. It was probably supplied by the Red Cross. 1920s photos.

Top photo courtesy - Halifax Port Corporation. Lower photo courtesy - CEIC.

assistance to those who were rendered vulnerable because of their temporary circumstances. Although the laws of efficiency required that people be quickly moved through the immigration system, most historical documents reveal that a compassionate approach was used whenever possible.

Recalling the heyday of activity at Pier 21, Alison Smith, now Mrs. J.H. Trapnell, concludes of the staff and volunteers who manned its offices, halls, and corridors: "They were all a dedicated lot."

A group of immigrants entertain fellow passengers during a Christmas party. Photo circa 1929.

Courtesy - Halifax Port Corporation

Under the
Yellow Flag:
Quarantine

Historically the naval activity of any port city has been inherently and essentially linked to that city's system of quarantine. This was especially true for the Port of Halifax where thousands of people from many parts of the world sought entry into Canada. Because the Port was for many years witness to such heavy human traffic, a system for the management and control of a varied collection of infectious diseases came to feature prominently in port and city activities.

It is known that in the forty years prior to confederation, Halifax had a system of quarantine in place. Although no regular quarantine station existed at the time, the **Pyramus**, stationed in Halifax from 1832 until 1879, was used as a hospital ship whenever necessary. The **Pyramus** was pressed into service in 1861 when four ships from the West Indies arrived in Halifax with yellow fever on board. When the epidemic had finally been contained, there had been 334 cases of the contagion, and 112 deaths, 52 of which had occurred in Halifax.

The most memorable case of cholera in Halifax involved the SS **England** which in 1866 spent a fortnight moored off NcNab's Island. When the **England** limped into the outer harbour of Halifax, 300 of her 1300 passengers had already died and more were perishing daily. Dr. John Slayter, the Port Health Officer, examined the ship and knew he had a medical emergency on his hands. He immediately redirected the **England** to McNab's Island and gallantly joined it in quarantine there.

Dr. Slayter's prime concern was to isolate the sick. The **Pyramus** was swiftly dispatched to McNab's Island. Four hundred stricken passengers were transferred to the **Pyramus** and the healthy passengers were removed to the island where they were placed in tents that did little to ward off the bitter cold of early spring. Once empty, the **England** was thoroughly cleaned and fumigated.

As the number of victims continued to increase, Dr. Slayter saw the burial of the dead as an urgent concern. He designated Thrum Cap on the southern tip of the island as an appropriate burial site. Although assistance soon arrived in the form of three physicians, a priest and three Sisters of Charity, the work at McNab's was exhaustive and emotionally draining. In his various reports, Dr. Slayter told of boatloads of bodies, and of having to row thirty coffins around Hangman's Beach to Thrum Cap. Once at the burial site, the deep graves had to be dug and then filled in again.

Eventually the dead numbered so many that convicts from the Halifax jails were forcibly recruited to serve as grave diggers. As the convicts, generously plied with the alcohol they had received as payment for the distasteful task, grew drunker, they became more profane and increasingly rowdy and careless in the handling of the dead. One of the volunteer Sisters was later moved to remark that, "It was easy to meditate on hell in those days."

In an attempt to confine the cholera to McNab's Island, four policemen were dispatched in a boat to patrol the waters around the island. Dr. Slayter had serious questions about their usefulness, especially after several of the quarantined passengers managed to escape to the mainland. Finally an army regiment was sent to the island to ensure that a quarantine situation would be maintained.

This too, however, added to Dr. Slayter's difficulties. The army proceeded to herd the immigrants away from their initial encampment, charging that they had been using the military buildings on that site without permission. The immigrants were banished to the southern half of the island where no shelters existed.

By this time Dr. Slayter was growing weary, although the epidemic was beginning to show signs of waning. He was being pressed by the city's health officers for reports he did not have time to write. In one report his frustration moved him to suggest to his superiors that they come to McNab's Island to assess the situation for themselves.

When the **England** finally continued on to her American destination, she left behind some 200 victims who were buried, some in lead coffins and some in mass graves, on the island. Ironically and tragically, the last victim to be buried there was Dr. Slayter himself, who, twenty-four hours earlier, had fallen victim to the disease. He was 37 years old.

Mere days later the Nova Scotia government awarded the sum of two thousand dollars in compensation to his widow. In December of 1966 Dr. Slayter's body was exhumed and reburied in Halifax's Camp Hill Cemetery. The following summer Halifax saw fit to recognize his valiant contribution to humanity by erecting a monument in his honour.

In the wake of this ordeal, the colonial government of Nova Scotia recognized the urgent need for a permanent quarantine facility that would be unobtrusively located well away from the people of Halifax and Dartmouth. Their collective eye fell upon Lawlor's Island, a 200-acre mound of land nestled behind the larger McNab's Island. Situated near the harbour entrance and five miles from the Halifax shore, it was touted as the ideal location for quarantine and isolation.

After a lengthy attempt to obtain clear title to Lawlor's Island, it was officially established as a quarantine station in May of 1868. (Confederation had meanwhile taken place and the responsibility for the development of a quarantine facility had been transferred from the province to the dominion government.) However, the building of a quarantine facility on the island was further delayed and in 1869 the HMS **Eclipse**, with several cases of yellow fever aboard, was sent instead to a small island in the Bedford Basin.

In 1871 the quarantine station at Lawlor's Island was still not ready when an emergency situation arose that nonetheless required its immediate use. A temporary shed, the roof of which was made watertight with a covering of old sails, was erected within twenty-four hours. Although not much is known about this "emergency situation," it is believed that the first victim to be buried on Lawlor's Island was a seaman who had died of "consumption."

When the SS **Franklyn** entered Halifax harbour in November of 1871, yet another serious health crisis arose. The **Franklyn**, carrying immigrants from Scandinavia to New York, was in Halifax to refuel and obtain food supplies. The Port Health Officer, Dr. Francis Garvie, was not told of the thirty cholera victims who had died aboard the **Franklyn** and who had been buried at sea. He therefore conducted but a superficial inspection of the vessel and then allowed it to dock.

Shortly thereafter, two local suppliers to the vessel were stricken with cholera. One of the unfortunates was immediately quarantined in Halifax, where he subsequently died mere days later. The other, when he became ill, was taken to his father's home in the nearby community of Chezzetcook. It followed that several members of his family also developed the symptoms of cholera. Except for two cousins, all recovered. For a time Chezzetcook was placed under strict quarantine. All contaminated material was properly disposed of and in the end, the cholera was effectively contained.

This latest outbreak of cholera prompted the government to consider the development of a quarantine station on Lawlor's Island to be of the utmost priority. Over the winter of 1871 three hospitals were hastily constructed on the island, one for each of the three classes of travellers normally found aboard a passenger ship. The sense of urgency was such that the buildings were constructed first and their foundations were excavated and built later, in spring when the ground had finally thawed.

In April, 1872, and even before the completion of the facilities, two cases of smallpox from the SS **Peruvian** were sent to the island. One recovered from the infectious disease; the other was not as fortunate.

A permanent quarantine facility was finally erected in 1878. An 1893 government report describes the facility at Lawlor's Island as being divided into three sections and containing two hospitals, a steward's residence and various outbuildings. It is interesting to note that the report makes reference to "old" buildings, structures that would have been no more than twenty years old at that time. The report further states:

> Owing to Halifax being the winter port of the Dominion this is a very important station. The buildings on it, though old, have been repaired and new buildings are being erected. The old wharf or landing place, is insufficient for present service, and the erection of a new wharf on or near which to place sulphur blast and steam disinfector, is about to be erected.[51]

In the winter of 1899 a group of 2,000 Doukhobors arrived in Halifax, seeking refuge from persecution in Czarist Russia. During the journey an eight-year-old child had succumbed to smallpox. The Port Health Officer, Dr. Montizambert, was taking no chances with a group this large; consequently the SS **Lake Superior** and its entire passenger load were relegated to Lawlor's Island. (This was one of two large, separate groups of Doukhobors to arrive in Halifax in 1899; the other group sailed on the **Lake Huron** and were not subjected to quarantine.)

Since the Lawlor's Island facility had space for only 1,400 people, an immediate housing crisis arose. Dr. Montizambert, who himself had gone into quarantine with the Doukhobors, made an urgent request for building supplies and carpenters. The supplies arrived promptly enough but not a carpenter could be found who would risk himself to possible exposure to smallpox. When the resourceful Doukhobors indicated a willingness to build the additional facilities, this was promptly approved. In four days they had erected the housing that was needed as well as a kitchen and bath house.

In the meantime, Joseph Bernstein, a Halifax resident with a proficiency in the Russian language, had volunteered to venture to Lawlor's Island and serve as an interpreter for the Doukhobors. This selfless act served to alleviate the communication difficulties that were being experienced by Dr. Montizambert.

While at Lawlor's Island, not one of the hearty Doukhobors succumbed to smallpox nor to the sub-zero temperatures. In fact, when the quarantine station was briefly transformed into a maternity hospital, their numbers were increased by one.

When they finally departed for homes in western Canada, the largest quarantine effort in the history of Halifax came to a successful close. A spokesman for the Doukhobors had this comment about their stay in quarantine: "The exile was not at all to be compared with the rigours of Siberian banishment, but still three weeks spent there had been dull exceedingly."[25]

In 1901 nine cases of smallpox from the schooners **Thalia** and **Goodwin** were quarantined at Lawlor's Island. Two of the cases proved fatal; the island became their final resting place.

For the next several decades the quarantine facility remained unused and eventually fell into a state of serious disrepair. A new infectious disease hospital was being established at Rockhead in Halifax but it had not been completed and therefore was not available when the next crisis arose.

In March, 1938, the SS **City of Aukland**, a freighter travelling from Calcutta, arrived in Halifax. Two days earlier a crewman had complained of pains and had been prescribed castor oil by the ship's steward. The incident was not recorded in the ship's log book, nor was it reported to the captain.

Because of an unfortunate series of events as a result of several misunderstandings, the freighter was allowed to dock at Pier 37 and her crew were transported by bus to Pier 21. While in the dining room, Ali Tobaruck, the crewman who had earlier complained of illness, suddenly collapsed. He was taken to the detention centre where he was seen by Dr. Lyall Cock, the Immigration Medical Officer.

Dr. Cock immediately suspected smallpox and knew he had a dilemma on his hands. With neither Lawlor's Island nor any suitable quarantine hospital available, his options for a suitable course of action were sorely limited. His testimony at a later Commission of Inquiry on the incident revealed how he grappled with his decision to send the stricken mariner to Halifax's Camp Hill Hospital:

After this brief examination I went out of the door and told them to close his door and not let anybody in. I went over to the telephone at the same time, thinking what I was going to do, scratching my head, because this Immigration Building in the detention quarters is really a very vital part of this community. If this building had had to be closed, I don't know what the passengers would have done. The only thing I could suggest would be that they take them over to Saint John. No passenger boat could land in Halifax if the Immigration staff was quarantined. Then also, turning over in my mind, was the fact that I was not quite sure about the condition of Lawlor's Island for receiving this man . . . There was no place in the City I could send him to and I could not keep him there.

. . . The next thing I did was to go down to the boat, which they were fumigating. I also knew I could not send this man back on the boat, because it was full of hydrocyanic acid gas.[49]

At Camp Hill Hospital, the smallpox was quickly confirmed and the hospital was placed under quarantine. Immediate arrangements were made to have Tobaruck transferred to Lawlor's Island. Eventually four orderlies who had been in close contact with the victim were also sent to Lawlor's. Two of the orderlies developed smallpox and two remained well. A physician, nurse and orderly formed the medical team that accompanied the group into quarantine.

Ali Tobaruck died two days later and was buried on the island. The two stricken orderlies eventually recovered, although one suffered serious permanent scarring.

Meanwhile, the detention area at Pier 21 had been disinfected and the detainees being held there were temporarily confined to their own quarters. Dr. Cock continued in his testimony:

I also issued orders that these people be kept at the far end of the building and not allowed to use the corridor at all. Fortunately for us, this was on a Sunday and there were not very many people around the building, that is, guards, immigration staff and people of that type. There were no boats that day and that was really the only break we had in this thing. The people I was most afraid of were the kitchen staff down below, the kitchen staff and the girls who waited on these tables down below. The dishes were washed and boiled and sterilized, and the girls were all told to wash themselves well and they change their clothes before they go home.[49]

The day after the crewman's collapse, all of the staff and detainees at Pier 21 were vaccinated, for a total of one hundred and nineteen inoculations. It was also the last time that Lawlor's Island was to be used as a quarantine facility; its replacement, the new Rockhead quarantine complex, was hastily completed and readied for service. The quarantine at Camp Hill Hospital was eventually lifted.

According to Dr. L.R. Hirtle who was affiliated with the Rockhead complex in the 1940s and 1950s, there were actually two Rockhead Hospitals, located next to each other near the area that now forms the entrance to the A. Murray MacKay Bridge. The two hospitals were also in close proximity to the Halifax Rockhead Prison, an imposing structure that was built in the mid-nineteenth century.

The larger of the two buildings was used to house those who had been in contact with victims of a communicable disease. The entire crew of a ship placed under quarantine could be housed at Rockhead. The smaller hospital was used to treat those who were actually stricken with the communicable disease. This facility had thirty beds and included living quarters for the caretaker. The two hospitals were constructed on the recommendation of the Inquiry that followed the smallpox incident.

Also as a direct result of the 1938 incident, 20,000 people in the Halifax and Dartmouth areas received the smallpox vaccine. And finally, because of the prevalence of communicable disease in the Far East, all ships from that part of the world would, from this point on, be routinely quarantined and their passenger load carefully inspected.

Historically, the issue of quarantine and medical inspection at the Port of Halifax seems to have been contentious at times. Medical inspections of both ships and immigrants were time-consuming and tediously routine; it was not difficult to become complacent and perhaps even careless about the procedures. Prior to 1928, all medical inspections of newcomers had been conducted in Halifax. After that date the initial medical inspections were carried out in the countries of departure, thereby alleviating the congestion in Halifax to some extent. By many acounts, the inspections seem to have been quick and superficial, no doubt a realistic assumption in light of the numbers that presented themselves, both here and in Europe, for a medical evaluation.

The procedure for the inspection of an arriving ship was always the same. If the vessel was not flying the quarantine flag, she was permitted to dock and await the arrival of the various personnel who would conduct the inspection. Without exception, the Port physician led the procession of officials up the ship's gangplank. He was followed by representatives from Immigration, Customs and Agriculture. Next came the shipping agents and longshoremen. Only when the inspection was completed and rendered satisfactory could the passengers begin to disembark.

If a ship arrived in the outer harbour flying the dreaded quarantine flag, the Port physician was transported there by way of the "doctor's boat," a 48-foot, wooden vessel that was permanently docked near the Pier. For many years this boat was the **Salucan II**, better known to her small crew as the "Sally can." A ship placed under quarantine would be directed to Lawlor's Island.

Sadly, Halifax seems to have lacked in solid long-term planning with respect to the quarantine issue. This is apparent in the fact that Lawlor's Island, although intended since the time of Confederation as a proper quarantine facility, was never quite ready when a serious health crisis arose. Halifax didn't plan for quarantine, rather, it reacted to quarantine. And each time the crisis was successfully quelled, the issue of quarantine was filed away, to be thought of only fleetingly until the next emergency arose.

The completion of the Rockhead Hospitals should have

satisfied Halifax's need for a quarantine facility. Yet, within a decade of the hospitals' opening, they were collectively being used as a detention centre for the refugees and Displaced Persons who could not be accommodated at Pier 21. One wonders how, with Rockhead filled to repletion, Halifax would have initiated a quarantine situation, had the need for one suddenly presented itself.

Another routine procedure for quarantine control fell under serious scrutiny as a result of the 1938 smallpox outbreak. This procedure, known as "radio pratique," evolved as follows:

> Pratique was a licence granted to enter port once quarantine regulations had been fulfilled. Originally it was granted only after an officer had inspected the ship, its crew and log book. It was a time-consuming procedure and had generally been replaced by the more commercially convenient radio pratique. This permitted the captain merely to send a message under oath that his vessel was free of disease and had not called at any infected ports. The vessel would then be given permission to dock and the official quarantine form could be filled out. [13]

The Commission of Inquiry on the smallpox outbreak recognized the serious limitations of the practice of radio pratique, and recommended that its use be reviewed by the Quarantine Service.

As passenger traffic has migrated away from the ports of the world, and as routine vaccination has evolved into a health measure approaching global proportions, quarantine on the waterfront is no longer the life and death issue it once was. Still, measures to ensure against epidemics remain in place at all Canadian points of entry. Unlike the measures of decades ago, today's quarantine systems are well-planned and judiciously executed. They are a far cry from the facilities of the distant past — the sub-zero temperatures in a makeshift hut, on a windy, snow-covered island, in the middle of an icy harbour.

The Great
Depression

In 1929, an estimated 165,000 immigrants were received at Pier 21. Increasingly, congestion was a problem that resulted in frayed tempers, misunderstandings, and heightened confusion. The arrival of a large ocean liner meant that as many as 1,500 newcomers would flood the reception area at one time, each hoping to be promptly examined and issued the coveted "yellow card."

For a time, and in an attempt to regain some control over the examination procedure, groups of 250 people were disembarked at a time. Although this move somewhat alleviated the congestion, the Pier's reception area remained alive with animated pandemonium throughout most of the 48 years during which the facility stood ready to welcome countless new Canadians.

One recorded observation provides a vivid description of the scenario that was unfolded at the Pier on a daily basis:

> An immense throng of men, women and children crowds an interior starkly illuminated by overhead lamps. The multitude may easily surpass the number of a thousand. A certain cheerful restlessness prevails; everywhere there is movement. People are leaving the restaurant dining-room at the far end; others are on their way with their children to the Red Cross room or Social Services; still others stand grouped about their baggage in conversation or in queues at the ticket windows or foreign exchange bureau. The floor lies

ankle deep with orange peel and paper, and above the perpetual babel of children's voices rises the strident tones of the loudspeaker announcing heavy baggage ready for inspection. The medley of sound is punctuated by repeated vocal reminders of their presence by telegraph company representatives on hand for business. Intended as a place of rest and supposedly occupied by persons merely waiting to go aboard their trains, the hall is in reality a maze where some mothers are anxiously tracking down wandering infants and others exhibit concern for that next most important commodity, the family possession of bags and boxes; or, to use another metaphor, the hall is a turbulent pool where people pass and re-pass, eddy in little vortices, and are borne about as on currents which pour in from all sides like tributary brooks in flood. Lost tickets, hurried canteen purchases, vehement debates as to supposed destinations — these are spontaneous and local disturbances within the welter of the whole.[41]

In the 1930s the number of newcomers arriving annually dwindled to a mere one-tenth of the numbers of the previous decade. The era of The Great Depression had settled over the western world, ocean traffic had been dramatically reduced, and even the tide of would-be immigrants recognized that Canada was no longer the economic haven of the 1920s. Indeed, the demand for ocean passage was so diminished that several steamship lines slashed their rates by fifteen percent in an attempt to generate business. This announced reduction applied to ships such as the **Aquitania**, the **Olympic**, the **Belgenland**, the **Europa**, and **Levaithian**, and to many more.

As economic times grew increasingly difficult in Canada, the government drew itself inward and attempted to dwell on its own domestic problems. Jobs became alarmingly scarce and salary cuts were a common occurrence. Without the supporting social policies and welfare programs of today, life became exceedingly difficult for the vast number of unemployed.

As more and more men vied for fewer jobs, prejudice

and discrimination rose to the surface and cast its ugly eye upon the migrant worker who, to many, was tangible proof that work was being taken from "real" Canadians. The migrant worker bore the brunt of many insults and degradations that were largely induced by the tensions of the time. It was a difficult time for immigrants, an arduous time for Canada.

In an attempt to alleviate the tension that was broiling insidiously beneath a thin surface, the government established a number of relief camps where the unemployed could engage in physical labour for a payment of twenty cents a day. Still, organized voices rose to protest the arrival of any and all new immigrants, claiming that the labour market was already flooded with unemployed workers. In 1934 an organization known as the Native Sons loudly condemned government action to bring 3,000 Mennonites to Canada.

During this decade Pier 21 witnessed far more departures than arrivals. Many immigrants, bitter and disenchanted with their adopted country, decided to return to their homeland. Many more were compelled to return because they were financially unable to weather the Depression years. Still others left under orders of deportation, many to countries where they would find conditions worse than they had experienced in Canada.

It was an arduous time for Pier 21 and for the staff and volunteers who worked there. Gone were the days when the Pier was abuzz with the happy anticipation of people who had come in search of a better life. Instead, the waiting areas were heavy with a general feeling of despondence that enveloped workers and travellers alike.

"What a country!" one disgruntled British immigrant was heard to say, "Paper money and wooden houses."[57]

The deportees struggled against their sentence until the bitter end. Intractably they vented their anger and frustrations upon those who had to carry out the deportation orders during the final stages. Even as they were being ushered onto the ships they continued to resist, unleashing their bitterness upon the Immigration staff unfortunate enough to have been appointed as their guards/escorts.

Those leaving voluntarily huddled dejectedly on the

waiting room benches as they waited for the final act of their own personal tragedies to be unfolded. With gnarled hands clutching suitcases of broken leather and with scarves and hats pulled low over downcast eyes they sat there, their spirits crumbling. These were the people who had dared to reach for their dreams and failed. These were the people who had gambled all and lost. Their anguish was intense.

Not only was Pier 21 a stoic and unwilling witness to the departure of thousands of broken souls, it was also the centre of another controversy during this unfortunate decade. Since its construction in 1928, it had been and still is to this day owned by the Halifax Harbour Commissioners (now known as the Halifax Port Corporation).

No sooner was the building completed when the Department of Immigration and Colonization moved in to occupy the entire second floor. Since both owner and tenant were branches of the federal government, a formal lease was not drawn up and for a number of years no rent was paid. The issue of rent eventually became a contentious one between owner and tenant. Now, in the 1930s with the economy failing and currency scarce, the Halifax Harbour Commissioners was beginning to insist that a rent be paid for the use of Pier 21. A 1933 report reveals their dissatisfaction with the situation:

> Immediately after the incorporation of the Halifax Harbour Commissioners and, in fact, before properties had been put under their administration, the Department of Immigration and Colonization moved from the Deepwater Terminals, where they had occupied the whole of the top floor of the shed on Pier 2, to the upper floor of Shed 21, Ocean Terminals. From that time there have been from the Commissioners' point of view, very unsatisfactory arrangements or lack of arrangements, not only in their regard to their inability to obtain any rental for the premises occupied, but also in regard to their reimbursement for their expenditures in the maintenance of the buildings and the supply of electricity, water and steam.
> . . . The Commissioners have always maintained that this is very unjust to their administration of the

properties and they propose to continue their efforts until a satisfactory solution is reached.[4]

The issue was resolved in 1934 in an agreement that saw the Halifax Harbour Commissioners reimbursed for the use of the facility since its opening in 1928. However, the agreement stipulated that henceforth the owners would be responsible for maintenance and repairs, as decreed by the Department of Public Works. An extensive list of work was drawn up, which included the installation of storm windows, cleaning and painting, and improvements in lighting, plumbing, washroom facilities and the hot water supply. Occasional delays in the completion of requested tasks resulted in frustrating interruptions to the day-to-day affairs of the Pier, as is illustrated in a 1935 memo from the tenant to the resident architect:

> Would you please arrange to have an IRON BAR installed in the Immigration Detention Recreation Room over the iron bars which (sic) now serve as a protection against anyone escaping.
>
> I may say that between the points of the two bars there is approximately eighteen inches distance to the roof, by which any active person can make their escape and last night we lost a stowaway who succeeded in escaping in this manner.[44]

In March of 1939, the **Andania** slipped into the Halifax harbour and slowly made her way to the Pier 21 seawall. On board were thirteen-year-old Marianne Echt and her parents, two sisters and grandmother. The Echts were paying passengers and had travelled comfortably, but Marianne remembers gazing down at the steerage passengers who were quartered below. She remembers their bowed, kerchiefed heads and their weather-beaten features. She was prompted to ask her grandmother who they were.

"Oh, they are people who are much less fortunate than we are," the older woman had responded.

The Echts knew that they were among the fortunate. Their departure from Dansig was timely; already the turmoil of impending war was beginning to gain momentum in Central Europe. As head of the household, Otto Echt had been intent on guiding his family to safer ground and had sought entry into Canada. A druggist by trade, he had been admitted on the condition that he purchase a farm and remain on it for seven years.

As soon as the family was settled on their farm in Milford, Nova Scotia, Otto Echt made application to have his remaining relatives, a group of ten, brought to Canada. He purchased a second farm for them and met all of the necessary conditions for their sponsorship. However, one bureaucratic delay led to another and permission to sail tragically came too late for the group. When they arrived at the port of departure, they found that their ship had left mere hours earlier, and that war had just been declared. The Echts lost their ten relatives to the atrocities of the concentration camp, and Canada lost ten prospective citizens.

The decade of the 1930s was destined to end on a series of unhappy notes. On September 4, 1939, one day after war was declared against Germany, the British liner, **Athenia**, became the first victim of retaliation. Bound for Canada with 1,400 passengers aboard, including a number of refugees, she was torpedoed and sunk off the coast of Ireland. Most of the passengers were lost.

"Two hundred and sixteen 'war refugees' reach Nova Scotia," shouted the September 14, 1939, newspaper headlines around the western world. The *Halifax Chronicle* described the arrival scene:

> Two hundred and sixteen men, women and children, victims of Nazi Germany's ruthlessness, when a U-boat sent a torpedo crashing through the port side of the big British passenger liner **Athenia**, reached a safe haven at Halifax yesterday . . .
>
> It was 11:30 a.m. that the **City of Flint** slipped into her seawall berth. Lining the deck of the sturdy freighter were scores of the submarine's victims. First three cheers came from the survivors. Then they broke into "O Canada." Mothers held young children in their arms. Women and children were dressed in seamen's

clothing. Others were attired in kimonos or had blankets wrapped around them. Some of them were refugees from the very heart of war-torn Europe, others were refugees who had attempted to escape any pending massacre on the seas planned by Germany . . .

In the pier scores of Red Cross nurses and doctors were ready to care for the sick or injured. In the immigration building hot meals and new clothing were awaiting the survivors . . .

Sixteen cars made up the rescue train but there was only one baggage car. Most of the passengers had no baggage.[65]

Pier 21 was the scene of heightened activity as staff strained to have all ready for the survivors. Two hundred and forty cots were set up for the wounded and exhausted arrivals. Attendants with stretchers were available to help the injured make their descent from the freighter. As well, since most of the survivors were travelling by train to Montreal, a specially equipped hospital car had been added for the treatment and care of the injured while on route.

This was the first group of war victims to arrive at Pier 21, the first of untold numbers to come, many under the most difficult of circumstances. In the brief period before the insidious tentacles of war would reach across the Atlantic to caress North America, Pier 21 had but time to exchange her civilian mandate for a military one. Quickly she donned a new uniform, hastily she took on a new identity. Now, in full military dress, she was ready to duel with the devil.

The
War Years

Troops return from war on the *Samaria* (left) and an unidentified liner. Circa 1945.

Photo by Canadian Army Photo
Courtesy - Halifax Herald Ltd.

In the weeks immediately following the declaration of World War II, Pier 21 was readied for her part in the drama that was to unfold. As a year-round port on Canada's east coast, Halifax was to play an extremely important role in the movement of the Canadian military to the European front. Indeed, an estimated 368,000 troops were to be transported across the Atlantic in 300 ship sailings. Except for two small army groups, all would sail from Halifax.

As the Department of National Defence stepped up its activities to control the departures of Canadian troops, Pier 21 was given a dramatic makeover. Immigration was compelled to give up 43,000 square feet of space including a large part of the assembly room and all of the space that had previously been occupied by U.S. Immigration.

(It is known that the United States Immigration Service maintained a presence in Halifax since at least 1910, first at Pier 2 and later at Pier 21. Its presence in this particular Canadian port came about because several of the liners were banned from entering American ports, yet carried passengers who were destined for the United States. These passengers were therefore processed in Halifax before continuing inland on to their American destination.

As well, many of the arrivals who had, prior to their departure, received permission to travel to the United States, chose to journey via Halifax to Chicago rather than directly to New York. It seems that the indirect route was significantly less expensive and therefore more popular. The difference in fare — one dollar.)

In hammering out a five-year agreement with its new military tenant, the owners of Pier 21 insisted on a number of conditions: any construction work was to be approved and supervised by the Department of Public Works, or carried out directly by the Department of National Defense. Furthermore, the space to be used by the military was to be restored to its original shape and condition upon conclusion of the tenancy.

Meanwhile, the Department of Immigration was to continue its occupancy of a more restricted space at Pier 21 at an annual rental fee of $25,000.

Beginning in 1939, the departure of troops through Pier 21 was a common, almost daily occurrence. Under the Pier's portals passed a continuous queue of Canada's youth, newly recruited and smartly attired in crisp military uniform. Already they were being hailed as heroes, recognized and praised for their courage in volunteering to enlist for their country.

On the dock a boisterous festivity often prevailed. The air literally hummed with excitement as the young recruits made the final preparations for departure. From under their newly issued caps, their nervous grins were quick and unrestrained as they waited for the call to board the ocean liner that lay patiently berthed mere feet away. For many, this was excitement in its purest form. This was the chance of a lifetime to escape the mundaneness of everyday living on the farm, in the factory, in a small landlocked town, or on the streets of urban Canada.

And yet, the hideously obscene reality of war rose to greet some even before they had completed the Atlantic crossing. Others closed their eyes forever on the bloodied, swollen meadows of Europe. For a great number of the young recruits, these last few hours spent on the Halifax seawall were to be their final contact with Canadian soil.

The need for troop carriers was urgent and immediate. One by one, the luxurious passenger liners were briskly refitted and pressed into service. They were methodically stripped of their frills and all available spaces were turned into sleeping accommodations. The most famous and splendid of the troop carriers was the ever-gracious **Queen Elizabeth**. In late 1942 the **Queen Elizabeth** paid its first visit to Halifax to pick up

The SS *Olympic* was a famous troop carrier in WW I. Shown here in the 1930s, she carried up to 1,500 immigrants per voyage.

Courtesy - CEIC

troops and transport them to Greenock, Scotland, a major destination for the disembarkation of Canadian troops during the Second World War.

With 14,000 sailors, soldiers and airmen on board, the largest single contingent of Canadian troops to sail on one ship, the mighty **Queen Elizabeth** steamed across the Atlantic. Among the passengers were a group of 250 airmen who, several weeks earlier, had refused to sail on the **Louis Pasteur**, claiming that she was in an unacceptably filthy state. In response, the irate captain of the **Louis Pasteur** has sailed out of port without his passengers, thus forcing the military and port personnel to make other arrangements for the airmen. By their good fortune, they ended up travelling on the **Queen**.

Although the **Queen Elizabeth** came to frequent the Port of Halifax on a number of occasions, her arrival never failed to create an excited stir. The following note describes her entrance into the harbour:

> There is great activity along the sea wall when the words "she's coming" is passed along. This means that the ship has been sighted and the busy men, the stevedores, go about examining their gear and their tow motors, and the freight handlers and baggagemen are preparing for their day. The large ship draws nearer but she pauses for a moment off Chebuctou Head to pick up the harbour pilot who will bring her safely alongside near the wall where the tugs will tow and push the huge ship to her dock. The seamen from the deck of the ship will toss lines and soon the ship is secured to her pier. [22]

During the war years, much of the military's maneuvers at Pier 21 was shrouded in secrecy. Neither the public nor the press had access to departure timetables. Ships arrived and left during all hours of the day and night, travelling always in convoy under the protection of the navy. Only two ships were authorized to travel unescorted; both the **Queen Elizabeth** and the **Queen Mary** were simply too fast for the slower moving convoys.

Equally anonymous was the processing by Immigration of a large number of seamen who jumped ship in Halifax and sought entry into Canada. Many of these sailors were from nations that had been forcibly allied with Germany; others were from countries such as Norway and France, countries that were being hopelessly trampled by the Nazis. It was common to have these seamen apply for landed immigrant status and then enlist with the Allies in the hope of helping their homelands.

As well, the Pier was continually involved in the processing of groups of sailors who had literally had their ships torpedoed from beneath them in the vast Atlantic. Time and time again groups of dishevelled survivors arrived in Halifax by way of freighters and troop carriers, by way of almost anything that floated.

Although the immigration activities at Pier 21 had largely been interrupted by the war, the building did not by any means sit idle. Between August 8, 1942 and December 27, 1942, a total of 58,820 armed forces personnel on thirty-seven ships left Halifax for duty overseas. During this time as well, a great number of wounded Canadians were transported back to Halifax, to be received at Pier 21.

At one point during the war years, the reception hall and examination room were turned into makeshift army barracks. For a time an entire regiment was housed there, using the ground floor as a drill area.

Pier 21 was also involved with the more dubious task of processing prisoners or war. In 1940 prisoners from the German ship, **Graf Spee**, were escorted through Pier 21 on their way to a prisoner of war camp in central Canada. Perhaps the most infamous convicted war criminal to come through Halifax was the notorious Kurt Meyer, Regimental Commander of the 12th and 25th Panzer Regiment. Meyer, who had been sentenced to life imprisonment for his part in the murder of Canadian troops captured in France, was whisked off to the Dorchester Federal Penitentiary in New Brunswick. He spent six years there before being returned to Germany.

The war also brought to Pier 21 an unlikely group of ocean travellers. At the onset of war Britain had initiated a plan to evacuate British children to Canada and other British dominions. The impetus behind the plan was an inherent fear that Britain might eventually be overtaken by Nazi Germany.

British Guest Children arrive at Pier 21 in 1941.

Photos by E.A. Bollinger
Courtesy - Public Archives of Nova Scotia

The scheme was enthusiastically received in Canada and plans were made to evacuate British children to safer havens west of the Atlantic.

Initially, the programme was met with serious setbacks when the hazards of sailing a sea littered with German submarines became more fully apparent. Tragically, two vessels carrying young Britons were destroyed at sea. Parents, weighing the perils of the ocean crossing against the dangers of keeping the children home, hastily retracted their participation in the program. In the end, only about 3,000 children were evacuated to Canada in 1940 and 1941, fewer than had been initially estimated.

The arrivals of the Guest Children at Pier 21 were cloaked in secrecy. Alison Trapnell, secretary to the Officer in Charge, realls the time when she was on holidays and received a prearranged, coded, telephone message from her boss. "The package I've been waiting for has arrived," he told her. Alison thus knew that another group of Guest Children had arrived and that her assistance was urgently required at Pier 21.

After the war, many of the older children found it difficult to return home to England. They had been emotionally adopted into families, had experienced several years of school and had become accepted by their communities. Some had to be forcibly escorted onto the ship, distresed at the prospect of having to return home. Indeed, a number of Guest Children later came back as immigrants, happy to settle permanently in Canada.

Maisie Lugar was eleven years old when her parents decided that she and her two brothers, ages seven and twelve, would be sent to Canada for the duration of the war. Because her family lived in a British industrial town that was occasionally the target of enemy bombing, her parents were eager to see their children evacuated to safer territory.

For Maisie's parents, Canada seemed the best place to send their children. They had elderly relatives in Sackville, New Brunswick, and although they didn't expect these relatives to provide accommodations for their children, it was nonetheless consoling to know that the children would not be entirely without family while in Canada. As well, Maisie's parents, like most Britons, believed that the war would be over

British Guest Children are received at Pier 21, in 1941.

Photos by E.A. Bollinger
Courtesy - Public Archives of Nova Scotia

68

by Christmas and that the separation from their children, therefore, would be for a brief time only.

Maisie and her brothers left Britain in the early summer of 1940 and travelled on the **Cairnesk**, a small freighter that was later torpedoed just outside of the Halifax harbour. The three youngsters formed part of a group of sixty-eight children, one of the earliest groups to be evacuated from Britain. During the passage on the **Cairnesk** they were cared for by several Red Cross attendants.

Maisie has vivid memories of her eighteen days at sea. The **Cairnesk** travelled in convoy and occasionally the children on deck were witness to fires on other ships, the result of torpedo attacks. Maisie remembers that instead of being frightened by the considerable hazards at hand, she experienced a rushing sense of excitement at what she was able to see from her perch on the deck. Indeed, her most anxious moment had nothing to do with the war; at one point she worried that she had become hopelessly separated from her brothers, even with her mother's stern orders to, "stay together, no matter what," still ringing in her ear.

In Halifax the children were met by volunteers of the Red Cross or I.O.D.E., and by the "CORBs," members of the Children's Overseas Reception Board. Maisie remembers staying overnight "somewhere," probably in Halifax, and travelling by train to New Brunswick. In Sackville, she was billeted with one family and her two brothers were placed with another.

Maisie remembers her foster family with great fondness. They bestowed upon her the same kindness that was extended to the members of their own family. After the war Maisie returned to England where she spent the next three years deliberating about her future. When she came back for a one month visit with her foster family in 1948, she met her future husband and decided to stay in Canada. They were married in 1951.

Her older brother remained in Canada after the war, and her younger brother immigrated in 1965. Maisie concedes that the bond with their own parents invariably suffered as a result of their years in Canada. "We grew up as Canadian

British Guest Children are received at Pier 21, in 1941.

Photos by E.A. Bollinger
Courtesy - Public Archives of Nova Scotia

children. If you take a child of eleven away from his parents, he just won't be as close anymore."

Chris Nolan was almost eight years old when he was evacuated to Canada from Glasgow, Scotland. For Chris' parents, the decision to send their only child to Canada was relatively easy; his mother was a Canadian who had originally gone to Scotland as a participant in a teacher exchange program. While there she had met and married his father. Her ties with Canada were still strong; her mother lived in Yarmouth, Nova Scotia, and various relatives resided in Halifax.

Chris arrived on the **Duchess of York** in August of 1940. The ship travelled in a convoy and took two weeks to complete the ocean crossing. There were chaperones and attendants on board but Chris paid little attention to them. Instead, he grew into the habit of spending time in the out-of-bounds engine room. In the middle of the night he would creep out of his cot and make his way down to the ship's engines. The crew tolerated him good-naturedly, no doubt grateful for the diversion that young Chris brought to their mundane tasks.

Since the engines were powered by steam, there was always a plentiful supply of hot water on hand for making tea. Chris remembers sipping the strong, sweet tea, liberally doused with condensed milk and served in a tin mug so heavy that it took both of his hands to guide it to his mouth.

The **Duchess of York** arrived at Pier 21 with between seven and eight hundred Guest Children on board. It was in the middle of the day and the Pier teemed with reporters and photographers. Chris remembers being bewildered by all the commotion and being besieged by the photographers, "probably because I was the only kid in a kilt!"

The young evacuees were initially billeted at the Sir Frederick Fraser School for the Blind. To young Chris it seemed like a jail with its high chain-link fence. He was finally rescued by an aunt and uncle in Halifax with whom he spent the first winter. He then moved to Yarmouth.

Chris experienced homesickness, likely due in part to the fact that "nobody could understand me at first." He took part in a radio broadcast that afforded British Guest Children the opportunity to communicate with their parents. He also wrote numerous photo-reduced aerograms, letters that were reduced to postcard size and mailed as such. Chris remembers that deciphering the incoming aerograms presented no uncertain challenge, and provided a form of entertainment that could go on for an indefinite period of time.

After the war, Chris remained in Canada and was joined in 1947 by his mother who had been widowed in the interim. Today he lives with his family in Bedford, Nova Scotia.

On March 5, 1944, a raging fire swept through the halls of Pier 21, leaving in its wake nothing but blackened destruction. (Ironically, only two years earlier and as a result of similar installations in Britain, air raid and fire protection measures had been installed at Pier 21 at a cost of seven hundred dollars.) Swiftly, ruthlessly, it reduced a sizable part of the Pier to a charred shell. Alison Trapnell recalls receiving a Sunday morning telephone call from H.M. Grant, Officer-in-Charge at the Pier. "Don't bother to come into work tomorrow," he boomed over the telephone, "the place is burning down!"

The early morning fire was believed to have been started in a lot of mattresses that were being disinfected in one of the three steam heated Disinfestor Chambers installed by the Army in the Assembly Room. Miraculously, few people had been in the building when the fire broke out and no lives were lost.

When the last burning ember had been extinguished, the entire upper floor of the Pier sat in complete ruination. Port officials estimated the loss at $350,000. Two ships had been tied up at Pier 21 at the time of the fire. Fortunately, neither the **Mauretania** nor the **Scythia** suffered any damage.

In the aftermath it was revealed that realms of Immigration files had been hopelessly charred and entire pockets of vital information had been destroyed. Alison Trapnell remembers seeing the typewriters, ungracious blobs of twisted, tortured metal that had been melted into the desktops.

An immediate crisis arose. Pier 21 was not a business that could be closed while order was being restored. Accommodations for the Immigration offices were urgently needed; these were temporarily found in the downtown office of Pickford and Black. Mere days later, the Immigration offices were again moved, this time into the Pier 21 Annex, occupying space that had originally been used by the Canadian Pacific Railway.

Meanwhile, four wooden sheds were hastily constructed near Pier 21, to be used by Immigration until their former accommodations were restored. The Luxtave Huts, as the temporary sheds came to be known, provided office space only; all passengers and immigrants continued to be processed in the gutted Pier. The huts came with their own set of irritating problems: they were crowded and particularly beset with a chronic infestation of cockroaches.

Incredibly, while the restorations were being carried out at Pier 21, a second fire occurred in one of its storage areas. This time the damage was slight, estimated at only $6,000. Yet, with heightened concern over the risk of fire, the Port authorities discussed at length the feasibility of housing detention and hospital quarters in what was essentially a transit shed. To have people detained at the Pier around the clock added to the risk of loss of life, should a fire break out undetected during the night. In the end, however, concerns were quelled and the detention and hospital quarters were reconstructed as part of the facility.

In December of 1946, the Immigration offices were moved back into the newly refurbished Pier 21. Meanwhile, the war had been declared ended. Already the ensuing post-war tide of immigrants and refugees was beginning to surge as thousands upon thousands of people clamored to begin life anew, far away from the devastation of war.

Much has been written about the Second World War. It has been chronicled, analyzed, dramatized, criticized and soundly condemned. Its toll has been calculated in dollars and cents and in broken bodies. Its effects have been felt worldwide.

Not as well known is the vital contribution made by Pier 21 to the war effort. Like a stoic sentinel, Pier 21 witnessed it all: the departure and return of hundreds of thousands of troops, the coming and going of prisoners of war, the return of the wounded and permanently disabled, and always, the arrivals of souls haunted by a passion to find a better place to live.

Pier 21 was not an active player in the hideous game of war; instead she may have been more aptly described as an unwilling witness with a responsibility to uphold. Her duties were straightforward and without pretension; yet, her contribution formed a significant part of Canada's international role during the war years.

War Brides
and Refugees

R.M.S. *Mauretania* arriving at Halifax, N.S. on August 24, 1946 with War Brides. Also aboard were the Lord Archbishop of Cantebury and Field Marshal Viscount Montgomery.

Photo by J. Hayward
Courtesy - Maritime Museum of the Atlantic

The Second World War left Europe in a pathetic state of complete and utter devastation. Everywhere, the souls of the homeless littered a continent that lay smoldering in the aftermath of human carnage. Robbed of the homelands they had known and the dreams they had harboured, the countless victims of war despaired at the cruel and seemingly merciless hand of fate. These were refugees in the true sense of the word. And these were refugees who, by the tens of thousands, turned their eyes across the Atlantic in search of a haven away from the nightmare their own countries had become.

Immediately after the war the United Nations set out to establish the International Refugee Organization (IRO) in an attempt to begin alleviating the plight of the victims of war. These victims were divided into two categories: **Refugees** were those who could no longer return to their homeland, and **Displaced Persons** (DP's), a term newly coined after the war, described those who no longer had a home country to return to. Essentially, DP's referred to those who "had no place of permanence in Europe."

Canada, wanting perhaps to atone for its sluggish and dubious role in the rescue efforts of the Jewish refugees of the previous decade, promptly became involved. An IRO officer was installed at Pier 21 to tend to the many and varied needs of refugee arrivals and several immigration officers were sent overseas to begin the business of processing would-be Canadians.

Although her first priority was to contribute to the

alleviation of the plight of the victims of war, Canada also had self-serving motivations in her desire to play a part in the massive rescue effort. To a lesser extent, she too had felt the effects of the war. While her many natural resources had lain untapped and unused, she had weathered a severe economic depression that included a serious unemployment crisis. As well, Canada had come to recognize that her miles and miles of tillable farmland had remained idle for too long. Now, with the war over and with her economy recovering, Canada recognized her own desperate need for farmers and labourers. In short, Canada was a nation in search of new Canadians.

Canada had yet another reason for her early involvement in the rescue of refugees and DP's. Because of Eastern Canada's proximity to the European continent, and because of Halifax's salience as a year-round port, the voyage to Canada became for many the quickest, safest, most logical, and probably cheapest way to travel.

The politics of this situation are further described in a 1959 publication by Ian Forbes Mackinnon:

> To observers at Halifax, from the day in April 1947 when S.S. **Aquitania** drew into dock carrying a pioneer contingent, it was obvious that Canada had opened the door well in advance of the United States and other western countries . . . the obstacles to resettlement early in 1948 in the States were such that even the immensely powerful philanthropic societies there, while active in Europe in the distribution of relief, could not defeat the exclusive laws of their own country and make it a haven for all their protégés . . .
>
> Neither could the rescue be left to other possibilities of resettlement. Australian passages, for example, did not begin in a substantial way until 1949, and until, some months later, chartered vessels used for immigrants on the outward voyage brought back Dutch troops from Indonesia. South America rivalled in an early start in refugee reception, but the ocean travel required twice the time, and other conditions operated to slow down the movement there.
>
> The United Kingdom had played its part already,

the settlement in Britain of much of the Polish Army had taken place. In 1947 the British nation was itself facing an economic crisis, yet undertook the "Balt Cygnet" and "Westward Ho" operations, whereby eighty-four thousand were received. Nevertheless, when vessels first became available in 1946 after the return of the fighting men, the short haul of six days across the Atlantic to Halifax helped to give to Canada a natural lead over all other countries.

Thus it was that, as the clouds of hardship deepened over central Europe in 1947, a narrow but distinct band of brightness showed for the homeless people over the north-western horizon where Canada lay awaiting its new inhabitants. Canada offered at this time the most promising means of resettlement to the stateless migrant, in effective legislation, and in the hope of early and satisfactory transportation.[41]

In the months following the war, all available ships were enlisted to transport the Canadian troops back to Canada. For the people of Pier 21, it was a busy but not unhappy time as young men were joyfully and tearfully reunited with their loved ones. And yet, a poignant sadness must have reigned in the air as well. For many of the troops, the time had now come to set aside the easy camaraderie of the military and to assume a lifestyle resembling some sort of normalcy. It was a time for partings as well as for reunions.

Also disembarking from the ships were the long, long lines of wounded soldiers, many bearing the physical scars of conflict and battle. Some had limbs missing, others had body parts encased in masses of bandage and plaster. Many would never be well again.

There were still others among the injured who bore no outwardly visible scars, yet their destruction was perhaps the most complete of all. Quietly they sat, devoid of expression, peering out uncomprehendingly through eyes no longer able to serve as the windows of their souls. Indisputably, Canada had paid dearly for her part in the struggle to attain global peace.

It was in 1947 that immigration to Canada was officially reopened, although the human tide across the

**The return of the troops!
Photo above shows troops
returning on the *Aquitania* on
June 26, 1945.**
Photo courtesy - Halifax Herald Ltd.

**Larger photo shows troops
aboard the Queen Elizabeth
arriving in Halifax on November
19, 1945.**
Photo by J. Hayward
Courtesy - DND, Maritime Command Museum

Troops return to Halifax on June 9, 1946 on board the *Aquitania*.

Photo by J. Hayward
Courtesy - Maritime Museum of the Atlantic

Atlantic had already gained momentum. Indeed, the post-war impetus was such that immigration jumped from a scant 13,000 in 1944 to 72,000 in 1946.

Even before Germany's surrender, preparations were underway for the transportation to Canada of an estimated 48,000 women who had met and married Canadian servicemen during the war, and of their 22,000 children. The 'War Brides' came chiefly from England, Scotland and Wales, but also from Holland, France, Belgium and Italy. The movement of these 66,000 immigrants was a well-organized and well co-ordinated effort on the part of the Canadian government. The vast majority arrived in Halifax, gaining entry into Canada through Pier 21.

By 1947 the transportation of the war brides was in full swing, many of them arriving on the **Aquitania** from Southhampton and the **Franconia** from Liverpool. Some of the larger groups were welcomed with pomp and fanfare; others arrived quietly, in the dead of night, to be greeted only by a husband, an immigration officer, and a large, empty hall.

For a great number of these young women, this venture marked their first time away from home. Many who were themselves barely out of adolescence came with infants in arm and scarcely enough information about their new country to afford them expectations that were anywhere near accurate.

The Department of National Defense must have anticipated that adjustment to the Canadian way of life would be a difficult challenge for many of the women. In a 1944 publication, "Welcome to War Brides," a booklet that was distributed to each of the new arrivals, the following advice is offered:

> Canadians are very democratic and take a dim view of people who try to impress them. They are, generally speaking, energetic and fun-loving. They'll join you happily in a good-natured "grouse" but it might be just as well to remember that they don't like criticism based solely on the fact that some Canadian customs may be different from those of other countries . . .
>
> You will be asked hundreds of times how you like

Canada. If you can make your answer an enthusiastic "I love it!" you will make friends right and left. Canadians are deeply in love with their country — just as you are with your homeland. Some British people find the prairies drab and depressing at first, but the people who live on them have learned their beauty. Whatever you do, for the sake of your happiness, don't run down the part of the country you find yourself in, any more than you would criticize a meal in a friend's house . . .

If you are a good listener you will learn many things that will help you understand Canada. You are going to Canada to make it your home, to bring up Canadian children, to become a Canadian yourself. The sooner you make the transition, the happier you and your husband and children are likely to be. Of course you will be lonely for your old friends and for your family, and homesick for your country at first. It's only natural that you should be and Canadians will understand and sympathize; but — don't make too open a display of it any more than you would display your personal troubles if you were still in Britain. Keep busy and interested, that's the best cure-all![62]

"Welcome to War Brides" was but one of a series of booklets distributed to the women. Although all of the booklets were intended to provide some sort of orientation to life in Canada, one of the young wives recalls feeling particularly unsettled upon being handed a publication entitled, "How to Deliver your own Baby."

Day after day Pier 21 was witness to these young arrivals about to embark on the greatest adventure of their lives. They came properly attired in hat and gloves, some with children and some very much alone. They came from the cities and the country, from well-to-do families and from common stock. They came as strangers, yet they all shared a strong and intimate bond — their hearts had been stolen by military men. As they sailed into Halifax and walked through the Pier, their thoughts must have simultaneously dwelled on the past, present, and future.

R.M.S. *Queen Mary* **with War Brides arriving in Halifax
on May 27, 1946.**

Photo by J. Hayward
Courtesy - Maritime Museum of the Atlantic

R.M.S. *Queen Mary* arriving in Halifax with War Brides, June 16, 1946.

Photo by J. Hayward
Courtesy - Maritime Museum of the Atlantic

Clare McDade, who arrived from England in 1946, has poignant memories of her voyage and early months in Canada. With an infant in tow, she had the good fortune to be relegated to a semi-private cabin on the **Queen Mary**. Her most vivid recollection of the ocean voyage is that, "the nappie changing was the worst. We had to go down to a room about three decks below and wash the nappies and hang them up. You were lucky if you got your own nappies back!"

When the **Queen Mary** docked in Halifax, Clare stood anxiously waiting for the moment when she would be blissfully reunited with her husband. It had been one long year since their parting. Clare especially looked forward to introducing her husband to their daughter, Susan, who had been born six months earlier.

As a matter of policy at Pier 21, military personnel were on hand to escort each war bride down the ship's steep rampway and onto the dock. For reasons of safety and expedience, children and hand baggage were carried by the soldier escorts. Like Clare's spouse, many of the husbands stood waiting at the bottom of the ramp.

When it was Clare's turn to disembark, her escort gathered little Susan in his arms and the three of them began the descent from the ship. As she approached her waiting husband, Clare eagerly anticipated his favorable reaction to Susan.

"Hello, Fred, and how've you been?" her husband's voice rang out suddenly in greeting to the young escort, coincidentally an acquaintance from his home town. As Clare stood wide-eyed with surprise, her husband quickly recovered from his gaffe and tenderly welcomed his family home. Adds Clare with a hint of amusement, "We've often laughed about that since!"

Although it was then already 9:30 p.m., Clare's husband was eager to proceed immediately to their home in Parrsboro. To her suggestion that they stay overnight in Halifax, he retorted energetically, "Oh no, we'll drive. It's only one hundred and twenty miles!" Clare had just learned her first lesson on distances in Canada.

Although the McDades made a brief stop in Truro for tea, Clare remembers the drive as being long, dark, and solitary. When they finally arrived at their home at 1:30 a.m., her husband's parents and six brothers were there, anxiously waiting, as Clare recalls bemusedly, "not for me but for the baby, the first girl in the family!"

Like Clare McDade, Marguerite Turner of Halifax has vivid memories of her metamorphosis from British sweetheart to Canadian wife. From her home town in northern England, she was summoned to proceed to a bombed-out hotel in London where she would wait to board the **Aquitania** out of Southampton. Marguerite remembers the day well; it was her twenty-sixth birthday.

As the group of war brides at the hotel were being briefed by the Canadian military, Marguerite couldn't help wondering what she had gotten herself into. She easily recalls the bittersweet memory. "There were four of us from Leeds and in the evening we all sat in a corner and cried."

During the ocean voyage, Marguerite was so seasick that she never once frequented the dining room. She recalls the gratitude she felt when the Nova Scotia coastline was finally sighted: "I was so happy to see land, I think I would have kissed it!"

Marguerite remembers her pleasant surprise at seeing her husband in civilian clothes for the first time. She was standing on the ship's deck and he had positioned himself at eye level, on the Pier 21 roof. In a brown striped suit and trilby hat, he left a favorable impression.

In the years that followed, many of Marguerite's relatives immigrated to Canada. Today she has over fifty family members living in the western provinces.

Mary Bowser of Dartmouth remembers her arrival from England in July of 1946. It was a warm, summer day and she was surprised to find herself uncomfortably hot in the woolen suit, hat, and gloves that she had selected for this special occasion. Mary harboured no great anxieties about meeting her husband's family; she had been corresponding with them for three years and felt that she knew them well. They, in turn, showered her with flowers and gifts, and hosted a welcoming reception at the Lord Nelson Hotel.

Mary and her husband lived with his parents for two years, during which time they searched desperately for a home of their own. She remembers the housing situation in Halifax as being particularly deplorable, "You could get a room with an old wood stove and broken furniture for eight dollars a week."

During her early years in Canada, Mary received much peer support from a war brides group, organized by the Red Cross. Every Friday afternoon, the group of approximately seventy-two immigrants met at the Red Cross building which was then on Morris Street. While they sipped tea, they chatted, sewed, and prepared boxes of food and supplies for Britain. Mary remembers the Red Cross with fondness and gratitude.

There is probably not a war bride anywhere who would deny that she has experienced bouts of homesickness, of longing for family, friends and the old country, in the course of her adjustment to the Canadian way of life. For many of these women the homesickness, although it was never entirely eradicated, eventually faded into something that could be described as benign and controllable. As their new lives gained momentum, the old world was gradually nudged into a small corner of the past. Although it would always be referred to as "Home," it was no longer considered a home to return to.

For a small minority, however, the insidious homesickness turned into a mental depression more intense and paralytic than they could bear. These were the young women who, unable to cope, returned to their homelands, frightened, unhappy, and defeated. In many cases, these were the women who had had no idea of what to expect in Canada, and who were shocked and disappointed by that they found.

Clare McDade remembers a fellow passenger whose destination was "my husband's ranch in Peggy's Cove." To this day, Clare wonders whatever became of the unsuspecting young wife. Says Mary Bowser, "These were the ones who went back home. The Red Cross sent quite a few back."

Brenda Bennett was a mere seventeen years old when she stepped off the **Aquitania** and walked into the Pier 21 reception hall in 1946. Brenda well remembers the loneliness of those first few years. In England she had enjoyed the cozy

The arrival of the War Brides. Photos circa 1946.

Courtesy - Public Archives of Nova Scotia

90

camaraderie of a close-knit family and community. Now in Canada, she began to experience an acute sense of physical and emotional isolation.

Eventually Brenda and her husband succumbed to her homesickness and returned to England, intent on living there permanently. Being back in England gave Brenda "the insurance that it was still there," and her loneliness finally began to subside. One and a half years later, the Bennetts made the decision to return once again to Canada. This time Brenda knew what to expect. Her longing for the old life in England had finally been quelled and her homesickness had been abated. This time Brenda came to stay.

Ever since Joy Wilson married her Canadian husband in 1941, she had wanted to come to Canada. Even his death in 1942 did not dissuade her intentions, although it did drastically change her immediate plans. In 1948, she and her young son boarded the **Aquitania** for a four-month visit with her late husband's parents in Toronto.

Joy recalls her first time in the ship's dining room; she remembers feasting her eyes on baskets of fresh white rolls such as she had not seen since before the war. "It was like a fairy land and it was the first time my son had seen an orange!"

Joy's son immigrated to Canada in 1965; she herself finally came to stay in 1974.

Concurrent with the arrival of the war brides in the 1940s was the more sobering flood of refugees and Displaced Persons who came streaming into the Pier 21 facility in one final, desperate attempt to change the nightmare their destinies had become. It has been estimated that of the 500,000 immigrants who came through Halifax in the years following the war, at least 100,000 were refugees and DP's.

The refugees came from the oppressed countries of Europe — the Ukraine, Czechoslovakia, Yugoslavia, Hungary, Italy and Austria. They were labourers and professionals alike, intimately bonded by their inability to return to a homeland that would never be the same again. They were Lutherans, Jews, Hussites, Mennonites, and Evangelicals. A majority of them were Roman Catholic because the countries that had been crushed by Nazi and Communist forces had traditionally been Catholic.

Most came with few possessions, many with only an ill-fitting set of borrowed clothing on their backs. They huddled in small groups, knowing that the provisional visas they had been issued by immigration personnel while still in Europe meant only that they had been able to comply with initial admission regulations. Final admission, for which there was no guarantee, would be granted only at the port of entry. For many, an agonizing eternity must have passed before the coveted yellow pass was finally issued.

For many of the older refugees, the strains of war proved too great a burden; they had survived loss of or separation from family, they were without funds, they had endured famine and persecution, and they had left behind an unrecognizable homeland. Now they found themselves as part of a raucous crowd in a noisy hall, penniless, without language, and alone in an alien world. Their acute despair was evidenced by a "species of fright which even the kindness of train officials was unable to allay."[41]

Not all of the refugees gained entry into Canada. Although benevolence was exercised whenever possible, a small number failed to meet the requirements for landed immigrant status and were subsequently deported back to Europe. A fear that gripped families and groups travelling together was the possible rejection of one or more of their members. (An individual could be denied entry into Canada because of a criminal record or the presence of communicable disease, or on the grounds of "moral turpitude." However, a deportation order was always preceded by a hearing at which time an individual could appeal his case.)

Some of the refugees created their own difficulties by being less than truthful with the immigration personnel. At the gateway to Canada they continued to practise the same deception that had served them so well in the past. Many had survived to this point only because of their cunning ability to take advantage of every situation, legal or otherwise. Although they risked deportation by doing so, they gave false information, invented street addresses of supposed sponsors in

Canada, and generally tried to present as good a case as they could for themselves and for their families.

In many instances, the motives for deception were not selfish. A harried father who had managed to keep his tattered family intact until now would have been driven to deception by a desperation borne out of love for his dependents. Indeed, his motives may have bordered on nobleness as he risked all to rally around the older and weaker members of his family, those whose entry into Canada would not have been as imminent.

The question, "How much money do you have?" often left the few refugees with funds frightened and puzzled about the intentions of the immigration personnel. Many had bought their way to freedom, paying off European guards and officials along the way. Would even their last few precious dollars be taken from them now, here in Canada? In some cases, it took a considerable amount of convincing before the refugees were made to realize that the immigration personnel were not interested in TAKING their money, only in ascertaining that it would be enough to see them through their first months in Canada.

Many of the refugees arrived without the financial means to take them any further than Halifax. The Sisters of Service came to their rescue with an appeal to the public for the establishment of an "immigration fund." Money from the fund was distributed to impoverished refugees arriving at the Pier, thereby enabling them to buy food and provisions for the train journey to their new homes.

It was a time of hectic confusion at Pier 21. So many of the refugees and DP's were arriving without money, sponsors, and proper documentation, thereby placing themselves entirely at the mercy of the Canadian government. To add to the consternation of the government, DP's also began arriving on their own, in small wooden boats, powered by steam and canvas and grossly inadequate in the role of passenger transport. Several of these craft were but small coastal vessels, less than one hundred and fifty feet in length, and ill-equipped for the long voyage on the unpredictable high seas.

The majority of the passengers of these small vessels were DP's from the overrun Baltic countries: Estonia, Latvia, and Lithuania. They had travelled to Sweden where they had paid for their perilous passage and thrown themselves at the mercy of the Atlantic. Throughout the voyage they were exposed to the elements and subjected to an inadequate diet. That most of them made it safely to Halifax is nothing short of miraculous.

The DP's travelled on the **Walnut** and the **Sarabande**, on the **Parnu**, a converted minesweeper, the **Ostervag**, and on the **Gladstone**, an old fishing schooner and perhaps the smallest of the vessels. All of the little boats arrived within a short period of each other, adding to the already heightened pace and confusion at Pier 21.

In 1948, the **Capry** limped into Halifax with 23 Latvian and 5 Estonian DP's on board. Formerly a British gunboat, she had been purchased in Sweden by her passengers in a final, frenetic attempt to seek safety on Canadian shores. Her arrival was timely — she had been at sea for 45 days, her food stores had been completely depleted, and but one barrel of fuel remained.

On August 19, 1949, the **Sarabande** arrived in Halifax, carrying a large group of DP's, including 60 children. The journey had been rough and perilous, and food and drinking water had been scarce. The *Halifax Chronicle-Herald* aptly described the scene at the waterfront:

> Tired, cramped and hungry, 238 Baltic refugees reached Halifax yesterday aboard the 183-ton minesweeper **Sarabande** after having left Gothenburg, Sweden, almost a month ago.
>
> Many of them still bearing the numbers branded on them in German and Russian concentration camps, the refugees, representing all walks of life, were eager to get ashore and get started on their new life in Canada.
>
> Last night the group was still huddled together aboard the old British minesweeper but immigration authorities said they hoped to disembark them today. After disembarking they are expected to be detained at the Rockhead hospital until their entry into Canada is sanctioned. Only a few had entry visas.
>
> Almost a third of the group are Polish. The others are from Latvia, Estonia and Finland. One Irish lad

who boarded the ship in Cork, Ireland, was among them.

Fishermen, tradesmen, mechanics, shipping clerks, they all hoped to continue the same lines of work in Canada. A Polish music conductor and a dentist were among those who wanted to continue in their chosen fields.[54]

The captain and shipping agent of the **Sarabande** had previously been warned not to engage in the transportation of "illegal" refugees. They were subsequently charged under the Immigration Act and fined four hundred dollars each.

Less than a week later the **Amanda**, a converted fish packer, was towed into Halifax Harbour by an R.C.M.P. cutter, the **French**. The **Amanda** had set sail from Sweden several weeks before, and had been found adrift 500 miles off the coast of Nova Scotia. The tiny boat was skippered by three Latvians and carried twenty Baltic refugees. Because of its size and the conditions surrounding its arrival, the **Amanda** created quite a stir and the occasion was given extensive press coverage. Even now, Stew Grant, an immigration guard stationed at Pier 21 at that time, marvels at how the overcrowded boat managed to navigate safely across the Atlantic.

It was Stew Grant's job to escort the passengers of the **Amanda** into the Pier 21 reception room. "There were close to fifty people of all ages on board," he remembers. "They looked none the worse for the wear and were very, very cheerful, pleased to have arrived. I think the captain had sailed by the seat of his pants!"

Like other immigrants, DP's arriving without proper documentation were held in detention until their papers could be put in order. While the government strove unsuccessfully to keep up with processing, the Pier's detention quarters were rapidly being filled to capacity. More space was urgently needed; this was found at the Rockhead Quarantine Hospital in Halifax's north end.

At one point, almost 400 DP's were kept in detention while their individual cases were being determined and reviewed. According to Father Anthony DesLauriers, Roman

The *Amanda,* left, and the *Gladstone,* below, were some of the smallest ships used to transport refugees to Halifax. Both photos dated 1949.

Courtesy - CEIC

Catholic Port Chaplain and Diocesan Director of Immigration at that time, the refugees "received the best of care, their health was well considered, and the food was very good"[22] while in detention.

Meanwhile, public sympathy ran high for the detainees who had risked life and limb in search of freedom. Many of the DP's were Roman Catholic who found much support forthcoming from their church in Halifax. Extensive help came from a network of Catholic organizations that reached far beyond the boundaries of Halifax. In a letter written in 1949, Father DesLauriers wrote that Halifax had been "DP conscious," and that over the previous two-year period not a single DP ship had been neglected.

There was little doubt that the DP's were grateful to be safely in Canada, even within the confines of the Rockhead Hospital. Within two days of the **Amanda**'s arrival, the detainees at Rockhead, including the passengers of the **Amanda**, held a thanksgiving service. A venerable mahogany table served as the altar, decorated with old egg crates, pieces of lace, branches and flowers. One of the DP's was an artist who created a life-size, charcoal drawing of the Lord of Calvary to position behind the altar. On another occasion, a makeshift Estonian choir performed at the local Lutheran church.

But the sporadic arrivals of these destitute DP's left the government grappling with the limitations of its own immigration policies. Should these homeless "displaced persons" be turned away for failing to comply with the proper procedure for immigration, or should they be allowed to stay thereby setting a successful example to others who would attempt to gain entry into Canada in the same manner? While the issue was being vehemently debated in Parliament, public interest and awareness continued to grow.

Then suddenly, in a surprise move in early November of 1949, the government announced the release of 267 detainees from the Rockhead Hospital. Meanwhile, another small boat sailing from Sweden and filled to overflowing with DP's, had been intercepted and was being held in Eire. The ship was the **Victory**, which had been designed to carry a maximum of 50 people. It had 385 passengers on board.

These two actions, occurring more or less simultaneously, proved to be timely and politically astute. The release of the detainees at Rockhead was met with public approval, yet generated a gnawing fear that the way had been made clear for many more boatloads of DP's to come to Canada via Sweden, rather than through the proper channels for immigration. The handling of the incident off the coast of Eire helped to dispel that anxiety. The message to the public was clear: while the Canadian government would not be hard-nosed in its dealings with a destitute people who had risked all to step ashore at Pier 21, Canada and other countries would, nonetheless, come down hard on the clandestine operation of the transport of refugees from Sweden across the Atlantic.

Among the poorest of the refugees were the Jewish survivors of the Holocaust, those with whom the mental images of the horrifying extremes of war would stay forever. The Canadian Jewish Congress arranged and paid for the passage of these DP's, many of them children who had been orphaned by the atrocities of the war. The long established Jewish Immigrant Aid Society of Canada (JIAS), was instrumental in the reception and resettlement of large numbers of Jewish refugees.

The Halifax committee of JIAS was especially active under the capable leadership of Noah Heinish, a well-known local merchant. Members of the committee were faithfully present at Pier 21 to welcome the immigrants, help them through immigration and customs, supply them with food, and tend to their general needs until their departure by train. Perhaps even more importantly, JIAS was there to welcome the immigrants with greetings in their own languages: Polish, Yiddish, Russian and German, among others. This gesture, even more so than gifts of food and financial assistance, would have served as a heartwarming gesture of welcome and hope, of reassurance to the refugees that they had arrived among friends.

One particular group of Jewish arrivals sparked considerable public and media interest. In January of 1949, seventeen Jewish orphans ranging in age from ten to eighteen years, disembarked at Pier 21. In the group was Ruth Miller

(Ruzena Meuller-Gewuerzman), an 11-year-old child from Czechoslovakia who had officially been deemed the 1,000th war orphan to be brought to Canada by the Canadian Jewish Congress. Before the day had ended, young Ruth had been presented with gifts and photographed for the front page of *The Halifax Mail Star.*

Incredibly, the children had escaped the horrible fate of their parents by hiding in the European wilderness or by living under assumed, non-Jewish names. They were warmly received by JIAS and well entertained at the Robie Street Synagogue before travelling to Montreal where they were eventually adopted into Canadian homes.

One month later the *Halifax Mail Star* announced on its front page that Canada had just received her 50,000th refugee:

> Eight-year-old Ausma Nevalds got the biggest reception of her life this morning when she arrived in the Port of Halifax on the **Samaria** — the 50,000th displaced person to come to Canada under the International Refugee Organization plan.
>
> The slight blonde Latvian girl was greeted in the Immigration centre by the flash and pop of camera flash bulbs, by swarming reporters and radio men, and her arrival was covered by newsreel men.
>
> Ausma was one of the 1,200 displaced persons from Cuxhaven to come ashore in Halifax en route to new homes in Canada. Accompanied by her mother Karline and sister Rasma, the little D.P. is en route to join her father, a farmer's helper in New Hamburg, Ontario. Their home in Latvia was the countryside of Liepaja.[33]

Ausma's arrival created a stir of excitement at Pier 21. She was interviewed by the media and presented with a doll and locket by Halifax Mayor J.E. Ahern. As Canada officially welcomed her 50,000th DP, the Ames' Brother record, "To Think You've Chosen Me," was playing in the background. For Canadians everywhere, it was a time to indulge briefly in self-congratulation, a time to acknowledge their country's not insignificant role in the rescue of humanity in need.

Eight-year-old Ausma Nevalds from Latvia was the 50,000th Displaced Person to be received by Canada. She arrived in 1949.

Photo by Norwood
Courtesy - Ausma Nevalds

Later in 1949, the arrival of yet another group of orphans attracted a great deal of public attention. This time the children were Polish, ranging in age from two to twenty, and orphaned when their parents had been deported to Russia. In their search for freedom, the children had survived an incredible journey from Europe to North Africa and back to Europe again, the Polish government always on their heels. With the help of the IRO, the children were eventually put on board the U.S. Army transport, the **General Heitzelman**, and brought to Halifax. Seemingly, efforts by the Polish regime to thwart the orphans' escape had been successfully foiled. Yet, in Halifax and again en route to Montreal, furtive attempts were made by Soviet-Polish representatives to apprehend the children.

The outrage of Canadians was aptly expressed through the media, including *The Ensign*, which ran a scathing commentary in its October 8, 1949 issue, excerpted as follows:

Few episodes in history are more sad or more shameful than the plight of the Polish orphans who for nearly ten years have been harried from country to country by Russian oppressors . . .

This dastardly persecution has not only occurred in the Near East and in Europe, but continues at this moment in Canada. Those of the orphans to whom we gave sanctuary were bothered on their arrival in Halifax; and near Montreal they had to be whisked off their train at a suburban station to escape hoodlums awaiting them in the central depot. Since then it has been necessary to keep our guests under special police protection, and the newspapers have been asked not to divulge their whereabouts.

To top this almost incredible disrespect for Canadian sovereignty, the Polish Minister to Canada, Mr. Milnikiel, dispatched a note to our Government not to apologize for the conduct of his henchmen but to make what we are reliably informed were insolent allegations that the children had been "shanghaied" into Canada. It was Mr. Milnikiel's contention that these children should now be returned to Communist Poland so that the jailers and murderers of their parents could bring them up in all the hideousness of atheism.[53]

It is thought that most of the orphans were eventually settled west of Montreal.

The plight of the post-war refugees had had a profound effect on many Canadians, all of them ordinary people who had embraced these homeless, friendless victims of human conflict, and welcomed them into their lives. Louise Wolff, a former librarian with the Department of Manpower and Immigration, felt compelled to describe the refugee in a poem, the last few stanzas of which appear below:

An aerial view of Pier 21 (right). The SS *Majestic* was the world's largest trans-Atlantic liner prior to the Queens. Photo circa 1940.

Courtesy - CEIC

There are refugees as people,
Who wander here and there,
But there's always the refugee mind,
For which no one seems to care.
The Mind that becomes a refugee,
Is far more sad t'would seem,
Than the refugee that roams the land,
Without a home or dream.
The Mind that becomes a refugee,
That has ceased to see a goal,
Is the saddest ruptured spirit,
Because it's a refugee soul.[63]

In 1950 the Canadian government announced the repeal of the Enemy Alien Prohibition Act, a statute that had been in effect for eleven years. The Act had prohibited the entry of Germans into Canada. However, the time had come, said Immigration Minister Harris in making the announcement, to develop a peace-time arrangement for the immigration of German Nationals. The Minister did caution that extra security regulations would be enforced in an attempt to keep Nazi Party Members and Communists out of Canada.

As the 1940s slowly faded into the perpetual past, the tide of war brides and post-war refugees to Canadian shores abated, calmed, and finally receded into history. The never-ending throngs of people who had passed through Pier 21 had invariably taken their toll on the aging facility. Paint was peeling, plaster was flaking and an unmistakable semblance of antiquity was settling over the venerable building.

In the last decade the issue of rent had again been hotly debated, bureaucratic battles had raged over renovations and repairs, and two fires had been endured. The time for retirement, however, was not at hand. Instead, preparations were being made for a bursting surge of post-war immigration, a surge that would last a full decade and that would see traffic on the high seas as dense as it had ever been. The mosaic of Canada was not yet complete. The work of Pier 21 was not yet finished.

People of
The Pier

Women and babies from the *Anna Salem* in the Immigration examining room.

Photo by G.L. Wetmore
Courtesy - Public Archives of Nova Scotia

No less dedicated than its predecessor was the Pier 21 volunteer team of the 1940s, 1950s and 1960s. Although he individual volunteers of the 1920s and 1930s had, in many cases, moved on, many of the organizations of the previous decades continued to maintain a strong presence on the Halifax waterfront. The chaplains representing various denominations, the YWCA, the Red Cross, the Sisters of Service and the Catholic Woman's League — all continued to be well represented at Pier 21.

A newcomer to the Pier 21 scene was John Lugass, an officer of the International Refugee Organization (I.R.O.), who had been stationed in Halifax immediately after the war. It was his duty to welcome the refugees and assist them in their arduous transition from harried travellers to fledgling citizens. The challenge was considerable, the days were gruelling, yet, from the little that is known about Mr. Lugass, it can be gleaned that he carried out his duties conscientiously and with considerable compassion.

One Latvian refugee, who came with her husband and two-year-old daughter, remembers the kindness of the I.R.O. officer: "We came in February with no winter clothes or rubbers, and our little daughter looked very hungry and miserable. He took us into his office and sent out for cocoa and fig newton cookies. As long as I live, I'll never forget how good those cookies tasted to us."[57]

The last of the ships chartered for the transport of refugees was the **Anna Salem**, which arrived in December of

1951. This marked the end of the I.R.O. officer's duties at Pier 21. Shortly thereafter, he "surrendered his appointment, the I.R.O. safe was sold, the telephone disconnected, and this extraordinary chapter in the fortunes of Canada came to an end."[41]

Throughout the war years and in the decade that followed, interpreters and volunteers proficient in languages other than English were in great demand on the Halifax waterfront. (On one occasion the 27,000-ton liner, **Georgic** arrived in Halifax with passengers who collectively spoke thirty-two languages.) Two well-known interpreters were members of the community of the Sisters of Service: Sister Dulaska, who devoted a full twenty years of her life to welcoming newcomers to Canada, had a good working knowledge of several European languages including Polish, Ukranian and Slovak. Sister Florence Kelly was affectionately known as "The German Sister" because of her proficiency in that language.

In response to how she came to be known as the German Sister, Sister Kelly replied, "the name was initially used as a joke by the customs and immigration officers, who thought it was amusing that someone by the name of 'Kelly' would be called to interpret in German. The name stuck, and whenever there was a need for someone to interpret for the German-speaking, the port people would call for 'the German sister.' Many of the German people thought they recognized which part of Germany I came from by my accent, and would be puzzled when they heard my name! We had a lot of fun."

There were other capable interpreters. Mrs. Helen Stein spoke English, French, German, and Italian. A Mr. Morris Kohler, himself a refugee, spoke German and Yiddish. Two other linguists were Sisters Salvatine Liota and Mary Shoptak.

One Halifax philanthropist with a venerable history of service and dedication to the cause of the immigrant was the well-known Mrs. Morris Fineberg. Sadie Fineberg, herself an immigrant, spent the better part of four decades at Pier 21, her learned eye keenly assessing the crowd in search of someone in need. As a representative of the Jewish Immigrant Aid Society

Sister Kelly, the "German Sister," welcomes groups of new arrivals to the Pier, circa 1950.

Courtesy - Sisters of Service

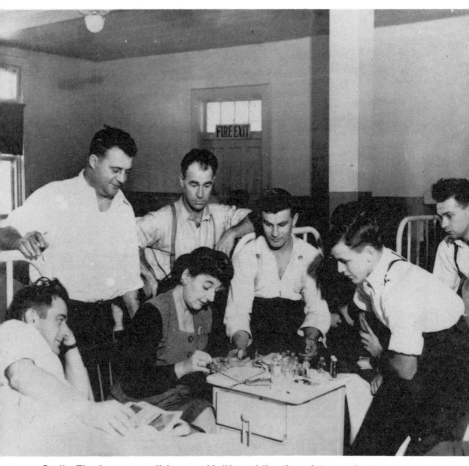

Sadie Fineberg, a well-known Halifax philanthropist, conducts a crafts class for convalescing soldiers at Camp Hill Hospital. Early 1940s photo.

Courtesy - Halifax Jewish Historical Society

(JIAS), Sadie was at the Pier officially to receive the many Jews who were arriving from all parts of Central and Eastern Europe.

Unofficially, Sadie was there to welcome anyone who could use a kind greeting, a word of reassurance. Her considerable energy coupled with her proficiency in seven languages made her a veritable ambassador at the gateway to Canada. A 1954 issue of *Chatelaine* described Sadie as "a talkative, open-hearted Halifax housewife," and went on to portray her as good-humoured, well-spoken, and brimming with energy. More often than not, she could be found at the Pier with a bulging pocket of facial tissue and armed with a loaf of garlic bread.

In Sadie's own words, the tissues were "to wipe the kids' noses," and the bread was on hand, "in case they're hungry."

Sadie's devotion to her work at Pier 21 was such that in 1948 she was given official recognition for her considerable efforts and contributions. In that year, Mayor John E. Ahern commissioned her "to officially represent the City of Halifax at the Immigration Piers in the capacity of greeter and counsellor."[1]

Sadie's considerable goodwill was not limited to the arrivals at Pier 21, nor was it confined to the Jewish community. Whenever immigrants, Jewish or not, arrived without funds and sustenance, Sadie would send for boxes of provisions from her husband's food service business. The considerable amount of food that went with the immigrants was always donated, and Sadie herself never accepted a penny for her services.

During the war years she organized in her own neighbourhood the Interfaith Goodwill Group for Aid to Britain. This group was instrumental in sending hospital and medical supplies to Britain, as well as Christmas treats and "sturdy boots" for British children. Sadie was also president of the B'Nai Brith and was actively involved in numerous other community and charitable organizations.

Sadie Fineberg in all probability holds the record for longest running volunteer at Pier 21. She was there in 1939 to greet the Echt family from Dansig, and she was still there more than thirty years later, on the eve of the closing of the Pier.

"I would like to take this opportunity to thank you for your kind generosity in helping to make more enjoyable the Christmas of those persons accommodated in our Quarters,"[42] wrote U.J. MacKinnon, the District Administrator of Immigration in a January 1971 letter to Mrs. Fineberg.

When Sadie Fineberg died in 1982 at 83 years of age, hundreds of tributes flowed in from all parts of North America. Her people, the countless numbers she had helped along the way, were sending their respect, their love, and their thanks. In their hearts, Sadie Fineberg was Pier 21. And in their hearts, she continues to live today.

When Mrs. Fineberg became Halifax's official representative at Pier 21 in 1948, she was succeeded as the JIAS representative by Meta (Mrs. Otto) Echt. Often in the company of her married daughter, Marianne Ferguson, Meta Echt could be found at the Pier, welcoming the refugees and immigrants in German and Yiddish. With funds from JIAS, the two women purchased food and supplies for those in need. Bandages and other personal items were procured from the Red Cross. The two women guided the newcomers to their trains and helped to settle them in for the journey to other parts of Canada. As well, they often brought kosher food to the immigrants who were being confined in the Pier 21 detention quarters.

Marianne Ferguson remembers how she and her mother would accompany the immigrants to the baggage quarters, downstairs, to help find and reclaim the heavier pieces of luggage. There were thousands of boxes, crates, and suitcases to sift through; Marianne recalls how she would pick up piece after piece asking, "Is it this one?" Rarely, however, was baggage lost.

Like her predecessor, Meta Echt did not limit her benevolence to the Jewish community. With her propensity for languages, she stood ready to help any immigrant in need of translation services, orientation, or simple reassurance.

Marianne remembers the destitute refugees huddled together in terror in the Pier's reception hall. These were the survivors of the concentration camps, these panic-stricken souls with the brand of death forever engraved into their arms. These were the multitude who had truly been to hell and back.

Using a copy of the ship's manifest, the two women would call out the names of the Jewish survivors. Marianne remembers that they would come forward slowly, crouching, with sheer terror written in their eyes. They lived in perpetual fear that the enemy would be lurking nearby, that the enemy had also crossed the Atlantic to infiltrate the Canadian system.

"When we told them we were with JIAS, they were overjoyed. Some hugged us," recalls Marianne.

Immigrants who were delayed in Halifax often found themselves enjoying the hospitality of the Echt family. Meta Echt was especially busy during the influx of the Hungarian refugees in the late 1950s. The refugees who were not detained at Pier 21 often went home with Meta.

Marianne Ferguson recalls that "there was always a certain smell to Pier 21. It was not unpleasant, it was like smoke, baggage, and food — salamis. I haven't smelled it since."

JIAS had other capable individuals involved at Pier 21 as well. Noah Heinish and Charles Zwerling gave "liberally of their time, efforts, and substance in receiving and sheltering Jewish immigrants." Both Morris Goldberg and Morris Fineberg could often be found at the Immigration facility. And finally, mention must be made of the efforts of Arthur Funt, a man who himself arrived as a Polish refugee in 1934. After the war years, Mr. Funt started to frequent Pier 21 on a regular basis, primarily in search of news of the relatives he had left behind in Poland.

Although he never learned the fate of his family, he stayed on at Pier 21, first as an individual volunteer and later as a representative of JIAS. Mr. Funt spoke English, Polish and Russian, and did much of his work with refugees and Displaced Persons. In later years, he was awarded a Red Cross certificate in recognition of the contribution he had made at Pier 21.

Another group that had successfully withstood the test of time at Pier 21 was the Canadian Red Cross Society. Throughout the years, the Red Cross continued to staff the Pier 21 nursery and, for a time, organized and operated a club for War Brides out of their Morris Street facility. The club, which had about seventy-five members, met regularly on

Arthur Funt (with hat), JIAS representative, with a group of refugees in the late 1940s.

Courtesy - Halifax Jewish Historical Society

Friday afternoons for tea, chatting, and sewing. The War Brides also became involved with a Red Cross program known as "Boxes for Britain," an effort to send food and supplies to Britons recovering from the war.

The YWCA continued to offer counselling services and helped in locating accommodations and employment for immigrants who intended to remain in the province. The YWCA also organized social gatherings for the newcomers, thereby providing them with a valuable opportunity to learn English.

Chaplains representing various denominations continued to navigate the corridors of Pier 21, ready to assist newcomers in need. Often this assistance was in the form of spiritual counselling and sustenance; more often than not it meant providing emotional support and basic physical necessities.

Father Pius, the Roman Catholic Chaplain of the 1930s, was followed by Father Ed Flaherty who served from 1942 to 1945, Father Anthony DesLauriers, 1946-1956, and Father Leo J. Burns, 1956-1968. In 1968 Father J.R. Brown accepted the post of Port Chaplain, a post he maintained until his retirement in 1986.

Father Brown assumed his duties with compassion and enthusiasm. Armed as well with an observing eye and a keen sense of humor, the chaplain stood ready to help any newcomer in need, regardless of denomination.

Routinely, the chaplain visited the seamen and refugees in detention, offering them socks, underwear, and toiletries. Maintaining that the refugee, especially, had to be shown signs of love and welcome, he often took new arrivals for a leisurely drive through the city. Father Brown recalls a Cuban refugee on one such excursion who showed a special interest in a men's shoe store. Realizing that the young man's own shoes were in tatters, the chaplain invited him to select a new pair. "As it turned out, he chose the most expensive pair! Fortunately, I had enough money to pay for them," Father Brown chuckled.

On another occasion, Father Brown was waiting at Pier 21 for three seamen in detention, for whom he had requested a day pass. He turned to a nearby RCMP officer to ask what he should do in the event that his charges attempted to escape.

Immigrant families at the Red Cross nursery.

Photo by E.A. Bollinger   Courtesy - Public Archives of Nova Scotia

The Red Cross sent boxes of supplies overseas during WW II, from Pier 21.

Courtesy - Red Cross

"Father," the officer replied without humour, "if they run, you'll save yourself a lot of trouble if you run with them."

One of Father Brown's most challenging cases involved his legal defence of three Polish seamen for whom legal aid could not be procured. At the initial hearing in Halifax, each of the refugee's requests for asylum was briskly denied and each was ordered deported. Father Brown immediately initiated an appeal, for which he and his charges were summoned to Ottawa. Against all odds, he won the appeal. The three jubilant seamen were allowed to remain in Canada. Today they are successful businessmen residing in the Toronto area.

During his term as Port Chaplain, Father Brown conducted many services for seamen either aboard the ships or on the waterfront. By and large, the seamen relied on the chaplain for spiritual and emotional guidance. Many were plagued with homesickness, mental depression, and general feelings of hopelessness, complex ailments that Father Brown attempted to alleviate during their short stay in Halifax.

The services proved a challenge to the chaplain, who has only a smattering of foreign languages himself. However, his ingenuity helped him to design a unique system that would enable people of many languages to worship together. Using his extensive collection of Bibles in foreign languages, he translated each component of the Roman Catholic Mass into nine different languages. The components were numbered and transcripts of the service were copied on coloured paper, using a different colour for each of the languages.

When conducting a service, Father Brown made available these transcripts as well as his Bibles. It was not unusual, he recalls, to hear the Creed recited in five different languages as worshippers were directed to "number four" on their sheets of paper.

When the large groups of Cuban and Czechoslovakian refugees arrived in the 1960s, many were temporarily housed at Pier 21. Most eventually moved to the boarding houses of Halifax. Father Brown estimates that he has been in every boarding house in the city. He recalls visiting a young Czechoslovakian couple and their newborn child. Asking the

Father J.R. Brown, the Roman Catholic Chaplain at Pier 21 in the late 1960s.

Courtesy - CEIC

couple what name they had chosen for their son, he was surprised to hear the reply, "Robert."

"Robert? After whom is he being named?" the chaplain asked, well aware of the European custom to name the firstborn male after his paternal grandfather.

"After Robert Kennedy," the young man responded.

He was astonished, the chaplain recalls, to hear that these people had heard of Robert Kennedy through their underground sources, and that they had secretly heralded his anti-discrimination policies, even in the midst of the stringent censorship and loss of freedom in their own country. Not even Robert Kennedy himself could have been aware of the far-reaching effects of his outspokeness.

On another occasion, a Cuban refugee was asked by the chaplain if there was anything he needed. His response was not the usual request for toiletries or cigarettes.

"Yes," the young man replied, "a piano."

Father Brown was so surprised that he recalls asking, "What colour?"

The Cuban explained that he was a professional pianist and greatly missed being able to play. The chaplain took him to Mount Saint Vincent University where he played beautifully for hours.

Such was the dedication of the Port Chaplain who walked through the halls of the Pier and who roamed along the windy waterfront looking for hearts and souls to touch. His concern was genuine and his kindness sincere. In time he grew to be loved by the refugees.

Looking back on a career that spanned two decades, Father Brown fondly recalls the many people who became a part of his life, who inadvertently shaped his attitudes and who reinforced his basic belief in the goodness of mankind. He chuckles as he reminisces about the four weddings he conducted at Pier 21, and about the funeral for a sea captain at which he was asked to officiate. At the conclusion of the funeral service, the good captain was soundly toasted by his survivors with a stiff nip of rum!

The chaplain acknowledges the valued support received from the Knights of Columbus, the Sisters of Charity and the Sisters of Service, the Red Cross Society, and many of the Halifax merchants. He also received many private donations, gifts of money and supplies that essentially provided him with an operating budget.

With regard to his work at the Pier, Father Brown concludes thoughtfully, "I'm very grateful I was assigned to do this work. Because what you get, you couldn't get in books; you get it through exposure, meeting these people of different nationalities, whether it's on ships or through refugees or immigration — their culture, music, everything."

Rev. J.C.P. Fraser often helped new arrivals with the purchase of their train tickets. 1960s photo.

Courtesy - CEIC

Another equally dedicated Port Chaplain was Rev. J.P.C. Fraser, who, together with his wife, served at Pier 21 during the 1960s for a period of ten years. Rev. Fraser, of the United Church of Canada, had, during the Second World War, provided much assistance to the men and women of the naval and merchant marines. After the war he lived for some time in Saskatchewan where he had supported returning servicemen in their attempts to re-adjust to civilian life. While there, he also provided support for many war brides striving to adapt to a new life in western Canada.

When Rev. and Mrs. Fraser arrived at Pier 21, they were already of the age when thoughts of retirement are normally entertained. Yet, the Frasers delved into their new commitment with unrestrained energy and dedication.

Immigrant children receive their "ditty bags" from Mrs. Fraser.
Her husband, Rev. Fraser, United Church Port Chaplain, looks on.
1960s photo.

Courtesy - CEIC

Because few of the immigrants arriving from Europe
were directly affiliated with the United Church, it had a
particularly interesting role to play in the receiving and
welcoming of newcomers to Canada. In the words of Rev.
Fraser, "We were therefore free to help those who needed it
most."

With the support of the United Church across the
country, Rev. and Mrs. Fraser distributed thousands of cloth
"ditty bags" among the steady stream of arrivals at Pier 21. The
bags, which were enthusiastically received, contained a wide
assortment of well chosen necessities: airmail forms, postage
stamps, notebook and pencil, soap, a comb, facial tissues,
toothbrush and toothpaste, a face cloth, treats for the children,
and a Bible in the language of choice. With the help of

volunteers, some of the bags were made up on the spot to fill a special need: a child improperly dressed for the cold might be given a warm cap or scarf, and a newlywed couple might find something appropriately special tucked inside their ditty bag.

The United Church had also made available to Rev. Fraser a fund from which he could draw to help passengers pay for their train tickets. The cost of the ticket could vary in accordance with the day of travel: a "red" day denoted the cheapest fare; both the "blue" and "white" days were more expensive. Occasionally, a family with a red day booking would arrive on a non-red day and without the means to pay the difference in fare. Unfailingly, Rev. Fraser would come to the rescue.

More tragic were the circumstance of the victims of unscrupulous travel agents. These travellers had been falsely assured that everything had been booked and paid for in advance. When they arrived to find the contrary and without the financial means to purchase their train tickets, Rev. Fraser approached them with funds and reassurance.

In the majority of instances, money that was borrowed by immigrant passengers was later unfailingly returned, arriving from addresses throughout the country. Only in rare cases was the loan not repaid.

Like Father Brown, the Frasers could be found at Pier 21 whenever a ship was scheduled to arrive, regardless of the hour. Said Mrs. Fraser, "There were many mornings we arrived home as the sun was rising."

During these night vigils, Father Brown and Rev. Fraser were also joined by Deacon Williams, the Anglican chaplain, now deceased. Father Brown remembers his colleagues with fondness: "We were like brothers on the second floor of Pier 21, waiting for a ship to come in. We were together on this."

In 1979, both Rev. Fraser and Father Brown were recognized by Employment and Immigration Canada for their considerable volunteer efforts on behalf of immigrants to this country. Rev. Fraser died in 1986 at the age of 96.

Another group of well-known volunteers at Pier 21 were the grey-clad Sisters of Service. They were known, not

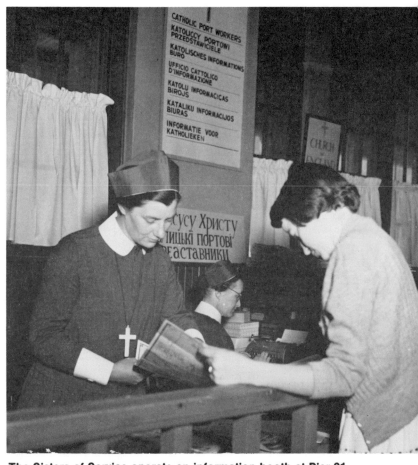

**The Sisters of Service operate an information booth at Pier 21.
Note the sign in several languages. Circa 1950.**

Courtesy - Sisters of Service

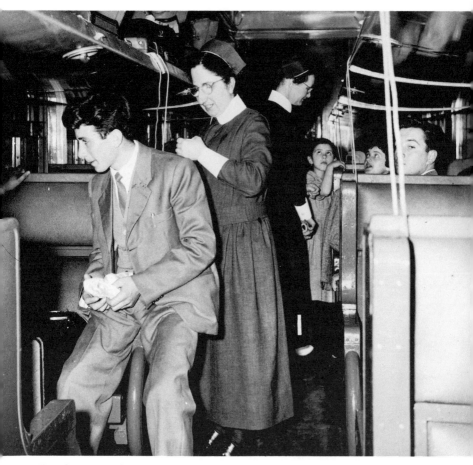

The Sisters of Service help immigrants to get settled on the "Immigrant Trains", circa 1950.

Courtesy - Sisters of Service

only for their considerable linguistic abilities but also for their compassion and concern for the immigrant arrivals. With the continued support of the Catholic Women's League and other Catholic organizations, they distributed religious articles and literature to grateful Catholic newcomers. Equally as much, however, they extended able hands in a genuine offer to help in any way possible. They acted as interpreters, gave directions and orientation, listened sympathetically, cared for the sick, wrote letters and sent telegrams at the request of the immigrants, and offered optimistic assurance to trepid individuals.

In 1985 the efforts of the Sisters of Service were recognized by the Catholic Church in Halifax. In paying tribute to their sixty years of contribution to a countless number of immigrants, the Diocesan Archbishop, James M. Hayes, remarked:

> Before Employment Canada existed, the Sisters of Service were the employment agency for many young women. Part of the Sisters' ministry in post-World War I was meeting the ships and assisting immigrant families to get settled in the Halifax area. They made arrangements for train travel for those venturing west to Toronto, Winnipeg, Edmonton, Vancouver. Often in other parts of Canada I have met people who remember as children travelling with their immigrant families. Not only did the Sisters provide lunch but candy and books to lighten the long tedious journey.[5]

Aside from the large volunteer contingent at Pier 21, there was also an extensive complement of staff in the 1940s and 1950s. Although these numbers began to wane somewhat in the 1960s, Immigration maintained a strong presence on the waterfront until the closing of the Pier in 1971. A 1959 publication provides some insight into the intricacies of the network of people stationed at Pier 21 at that time:

> At a late hour the employees of the five other departments sharing the responsibility of admitting immigrants have gathered up their paraphernalia, shut

**Immigration staff at Pier 21, in 1946. Photo taken
adjacent to the Luxtave Huts.**

Courtesy - Alison Trapnell

off the lights and closed up office doors; Health and Welfare, with hospital on the premises staffed by nurses; Justice, with plain-clothes Mounties behind the scenes; Agriculture, commissioned to confiscate all vegetable and animal material that might carry germs; the National Railway and its officers; the Customs Department, which at Halifax had the genius to place four of its charming lady staff in Canada's front window. These all, with the guards, dining room staff, shipping agents and others, were willing to call it a day — until the Camperdown Signals should report on the morrow: '09.00 hours: S.S. **Aquitania** picked up pilot, now passing Inner Automatic; on her way up!'[41]

Although the Pier 21 staff had little time to offer individual personal attention to the arrivals, it does seem that, for the most part, immigrants were welcomed and handled with as much compassion as time and individual situations allowed. Some of the immigration officers and guards made it a habit to give pennies or other small trinkets to the immigrant children. These small gifts, worth little in terms of monetary value but priceless as a gesture of friendly welcome, were eagerly received and cherished by the young arrivals.

Shortly before the closure of Pier 21, a woman presented herself at the guard office looking for a specific guard whose name she could not remember. As she was going through a detailed description of the guard in question, an unsuspecting Frank Wright sauntered into the office. Like his father before him, Frank had been a guard at Pier 21 for many years and had eventually been promoted to the position of Chief Guard.

"That's him!" the woman cried excitedly, pointing at Frank, "Do you remember me?" Frank had to confess that he did not.

"Well, I certainly remember you," she responded, energetic and unrestrained. At that point she called her son into the office. A lanky lad of seventeen appeared, wearing a chain around his neck. From the chain hung a single Canadian penny.

It seems that many years earlier, Frank had given a

penny to this young immigrant arrival at Pier 21. "Your first Canadian money," Frank had said to the little boy at that time. The boy had become so attached to the penny that his mother had finally arranged to have it put on a chain.

Now, many years later, both mother and son had come back to Halifax to thank the guard one more time.

Perhaps the most appropriate conclusion to an essay on the many people who manned their various posts at Pier 21 would be one that incorporates the thoughts and emotions of an individual who spent several years there. John Hood, now deceased, was representative of the People of the Pier — he was strongly committed to his work and genuinely enjoyed his responsibilities with Immigration. He aptly expresses the dedication of the People of the Pier in the following reflections, taken from his personal notes:

> It was in the long overtime hours voluntarily spent by seniors and clerks at the ticket windows, and in personal services to passengers at the baggage-room, in the dining-room and at the money exchange bureau, and by the railway police, by the 'red-caps' and men of the yards, that most of the difficulties were smoothed out. These men and women formed an amateur reception bureau; they watched over the needs of the passengers with such care that in all the tumult of moving vehicles and lengthy vistas of the open tracks of a great sea-port, in the passage of half a million people, not a child received an injury.[34]

The Tide
of Immigrants

A long line of passengers make their way into Canada by way of a ramp connecting their ship to Pier 21. Photo pre-1950s.

Courtesy - CEIC

On the heels of the war brides, refugees and Displaced Persons came a surging tide of post-war immigration, people from many countries in search of a new beginning. In the 1950s, Halifax welcomed an average of 45,000 immigrants a year, roughly one-third of the annual average received by Canada. This was the era of the ocean liner and it was not unusual to stroll along the Halifax waterfront and see more than one liner, filled to repletion with new Canadians, gingerly sidle into a berth near Pier 21.

Almost routinely, it seemed, the Halifax newspapers told of the heavy passenger traffic at Pier 21. "1,700 Passengers Land From Two Ocean Liners," read an April 1, 1952 headline in the *Halifax Chronicle-Herald.* The article reported that more than 4,500 people had arrived within the previous five-day period.

Father Anthony DesLauriers, then Port Chaplain, offers a glimpse of the vast mosaic of people rushing toward Canada, embracing her as a new homeland. In a 1963 personal essay he wrote:

> The gangplank is now tied to the pier and to the ship and the immigrants start the long procession to the shore. These immigrants are often from every part of Europe; they come from the Baltic, from the areas about the Black Sea, from the wheat fields of the Ukraine, from every country now behind the iron curtain, from the cities and the provinces of Italy, from

the fishing villages of Brittany, from the overflooded dykelands of Holland, from the industrial and congested cities of England, from the mountains of Austria and from the mines of Belgium. The newcomers to Canada are from all stages of life; they are the aged couple who came down the gangplank with difficulty supporting each other. Then come the army of youth, then the mothers holding their children by the hands.[22]

The manifest or ship's passenger list often revealed the presence of passengers of many nationalities. One ship arrived with such a varied assemblage of passengers that fifteen languages were spoken on board.

Unlike the refugees and Displaced Persons, many of the immigrants arrived with their families and carefully selected possessions intact. Their move had been well calculated in advance; they came in search of a new beginning and looked for reassurance that their adopted country had been wisely chosen. Into Pier 21 they spilled, clutching documents, baggage and children. Some chattered rapidly, their senses quickened, their excitement heightened. Others sat in silent trepidation, fearful of the unknown future.

A large number of Dutch emigrants came to Canada between 1947 and 1949. The Second World War had left the tiny country of Holland in a state of devastation, unable to offer a future in farming to its land-hungry population. It is estimated that Holland had a surplus of fifty thousand farmers in the early 1950s.

Canada, on the other hand, was eager to welcome able farmers who would till the vast farmland that had lain unused for so long. Canada was in need of capable agriculturists, and Holland had an unmanageable surplus. A cooperative arrangement to satisfy the needs of both countries was imminent.

The government of the Netherlands readily approved the emigration of its citizens and the Canadian government paid for the passage of many. As was the case with many other immigrants, the Dutch arrivals were placed with Canadian sponsors for a one-year period, after which time they supposedly would have saved enough funds to venture out on their own.

A unique feature of the cooperative arrangement between the two countries was that the government of the Netherlands continued to display an interest in its emigrants, even after thay had settled in Canada. Between 1953 and 1968, Holland had a representative on hand at the Pier to welcome the Dutch to Canada. It is interesting to note that this official, a Mr. W.V. Stoel, ultimately chose to remain in Canada, and retired in Richmond, British Columbia.

The Dutch arrivals became known for the large wooden crates they brought with them, forerunners perhaps, of the modern shipping container. These heavy and ungainly crates contained all of their worldly belongings. Pier 21 officials used to joke that the crates contained everything but the kitchen sink. The joking stopped on the day a crate was routinely opened to reveal a large, gleaming kitchen sink nestled among the household goods.

There was good reason for the immigrants from Holland to bring with them a veritable boatload of possessions. The Dutch government had decreed that the emigrants must leave their currency behind, save for one hundred dollars per adult and fifty dollars per child. Since there was no such restriction on goods, the resourceful Dutch translated much of their money into possessions which they packed in preparation for life in the new world.

There were many immigrants who were less prosperous than the Dutch. The poorer immigrants brought with them clothing and simple tools, anything they deemed to be of use to them in Canada. One family brought an old kitchen stove, another carried parts of a fireplace. They came, not with crates of linen and china, but with their own prized repertoire of dependable household possessions — an ancient sewing machine, feather matresses, cook pots and children's beds.

There were some who carried nothing but a battered valise; others arrived in borrowed clothing. Some came brimming with optimism; a few were greeted upon arrival by the ugly gargoyle of tragedy. In January, 1953, an elderly couple and their adult son disembarked at Pier 21, intent upon settling in British Columbia. The mother was confined to a wheelchair and the ailing father was left weakened from the effort of lifting suitcases and other baggage. Ten minutes before their train was scheduled to leave Halifax, the man sat down, collapsed and died. The grieving mother and son remained in Halifax overnight and chose to continue on to their destination the following day. They had come this far, they could not falter in their intentions now.

Immigrants from Italy began to arrive after 1948. Father Anthony DesLauriers considered the Italians to be "the greatest letter writers, telegram senders and telephone users that pass through this port." An immigrant from Germany remembers seeing a group of Italians at Pier 21, laden with ethnic delicacies and dozens of new shoes.

The Italian immigrants sailed to Canada on such ships as the **Vulcania**, the **Leonardo De Vinci**, and the **Cristoforo Columbo**. They were faithfully greeted upon their arrival by Angelo Rorai, the energetic Italian Vice-Consul in Halifax. Himself an immigrant from Italy, Mr. Rorai had arrived in Halifax in 1920 with a meagre twenty dollars in his pocket. As Vice-Consul he unfailingly met every ship of Italian registry over a twenty-five year period. His work on behalf of Italian immigrants to Canada was recognized in 1969 by the Pope, head of the Roman Catholic Church.

The movement of immigrants from Italy to Canada was considerable: in one year alone, thirty thousand Italians crossed the Atlantic to dock in Halifax.

One such immigrant was Felice Catalano who arrived on the **Saturnia** in 1956 at the age of 26. To this day he holds a poignant memory of his experience at Pier 21: "They kept me in Immigration for five days. I was scared because they kept me in this room with ten people and there were bunk beds. I had never seen bunk beds before. They said, 'Stay here and we will come back for you later,' and closed the steel door. I said, 'I never killed anybody, what is going on here?' Next morning we were let out for breakfast. It was the first time I saw corn flakes and bacon and eggs."

Although he was a barber by trade, Felice eagerly took the first job available, that of a labourer with a construction company. A worker's strike mere weeks later convinced him to set aside board and brick and to pursue his chosen trade instead. Since 1968, he has been happily settled at St. Mary's University Barber Shop where a loyal clientele keep him busy. Among his customers are the members of the U.S. Marine Band. When in Halifax, they converge upon Felice, looking for, "our barber, the only guy in town to give real marine haircuts."

Helene Saly vividly remembers her arrival in Halifax in 1951. In a 1981 letter written from Westmount, Quebec, she recalled the foggy morning in October when the **Anna Salem** slowly glided into the Halifax harbour. Cradling her sixteen-month-old son in her arms, she stood on the ship's upper deck, her emotions a tumultuous mixture of hope and anxiety.

Suddenly the boy took off his cap and tossed it on the water. As Mrs. Saly watched it float away, two observant dock workers jumped into a motorboat in pursuit of the cap. Although they failed to retrieve it, the kind and supportive gesture filled the Saly family with the comfort and encouragement needed to adjust to life in an alien country.

Mrs. Saly remembers that although Pier 21 offered little hint of the luxury that could be found in Canada, its reception of the immigrants was simple, efficient, and well conducted. This, she wrote, provided considerable comfort to those who were fleeing the consequences of the war.

Thirteen-year-old Konstant (Konny) Trus arrived in 1951 in the company of his parents and an older brother, en route to a new life in northern Alberta. They were from the Ukraine, a country that suffered total annihilation at the hands of both Russia and Nazi Germany. Their decade-long flight to freedom was a harrowing tale filled with the sordid details of forced labour, scavenging for food, unrelentless persecution, and sheltering in the gruesome crematoria of Germany. Konny remembers the poverty of his family upon their arrival at Pier 21. Except for the clothes they wore, they were essentially without money and possessions.

In the mid 1980s, Konny, now manager at RA Parks Officers' Mess in Halifax, and his wife celebrated their twenty-fifth wedding anniversary. To mark the occasion in a memorable way, their children made surprise arrangements for family and friends to visit Pier 21. There the arrival of the Trus family three decades earlier was poignantly reconstructed and commemorated. The occasion helped to reaffirm Konny's gratitude for his adopted country.

Robert Dietz departed Germany for Canada in the winter of 1951. He reminisced about his experiences in a 1984 article that appeared in the *Southender:*

> After the war I emigrated to Canada, arriving in Halifax on December 12, 1951. We stayed in the immigration quarters on Pier 20. All we could see from the windows was wooden houses and snow. We thought; "Out of the frying pan, into the fire! We just left Russia and now we're back again!" We had only ever seen wooden houses in Russia.
>
> We could not leave the immigration quarters until we had a job. Looking for one before Christmas would be difficult, we felt. Then we saw people shovelling snow, and we asked if we could do that — you didn't need English for that. CN was looking for people to shovel snow from the front of the Hotel Nova Scotian, so we did that. Then I got a job putting grease on the switches in the CN railyard. And I saw some beautiful silver spruce trees, growing wild in the forest. In Germany these trees are protected. I thought: "At home we can only buy such trees in stores. Here they grow wild in the forest!"
>
> So I cut down a tree to take back to the inmates in the immigration quarters so that we could have a silver TANNENBAUM. We lived 20 to a room and put the Christmas tree up in the cafeteria.
>
> The immigration officer noticed it. I told him that if he wanted one, I could get more for him.
>
> He asked where I had found it, and when I described the place, he said: "That's Point Pleasant Park." Then he asked me if anyone had seen me cutting down the tree. When I said that no one had seen me, he suggested that I keep quiet about the place where I'd "found" our tree.
>
> We were allowed to visit Halifax.

Robert Dietz documented
his immigration to Halifax
in December of 1951 with
these photographs. Above
is prior to his departure
from Bremerhafen, Germany.
Right, on board the
SS *Columbia*.

There it is!
We are here!

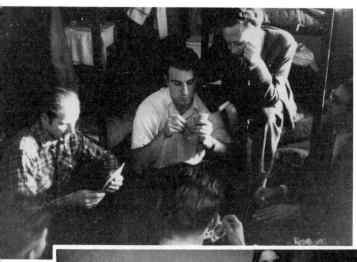

TOP PHOTO: **Thirty of the 800 arrivals were detained at Pier 21 while their papers were put in order.** ABOVE: **the couple on the left were eventually deported. He was Armenian, a nationality not welcome at that time.**

All photos courtesy - Robert Dietz

Around the time of Christmas, as we walked along Barrington Street towards the intersection with Spring Garden Road I heard a band playing the German national anthem — DEUTSCHLAND UBER ALLES. It was the Salvation Army Band, playing a hymn based on the same Haydn melody.

At the corner I noticed two churches, but could not decide which was the Catholic one. I saw the words "One Baptism" on Saint Mary's Basilica and thought that must be a Baptist church.

But we entered it.

As we did so, the priest celebrating the mass turned around, and said: "DOMINUS VOBISCUM — The Lord be with you."

I turned to my companions, saying; "ET CUM SPIRITU TUO."

And we felt at home.

And so in Canada, on my first Christmas, my first real contact with my new country was through music and language, the same here as "at home," throughout Canada and wherever people celebrate Christmas.[23]

Robert Dietz hastens to explain that his short period in the Pier 21 detention quarters was a pleasant experience. Detention was largely for those who had to wait while their documents were put in order, or who were unable to support themselves. In the latter case, most of the detainees left Pier 21 as soon as they had found work. Detention, notes Robert Dietz, was generally for one's own good. If an immigrant arrived penniless and without any knowledge of the English language, Pier 21 was the best place for him until he could get on his own two feet. The detention quarters were very much unlike prison in that a day pass to leave the Pier could be procured. "We were happy, we had shelter, food and kind and friendly immigration officers . . . We felt protected, sheltered, not jailed."

In the December of 1957, the Greek Liner **Queen Frederica** braved wintry seas and steamed diligently toward Halifax. On board was Barbara Campbell, a native of

Germany who had married a man employed with the Canadian Armed Forces. Her husband was returning home from a three-year posting in Germany, and she was leaving the country of her birth to accompany him.

"I felt excitement but this excitement was mixed with a great deal of apprehension. How will this country compare to my native Germany? Will I be able to adjust to this new environment, and will I ever be able to speak their language?"

It was a cold, dreary day when the **Queen Frederica** docked, and Barbara remembers that Halifax looked peaceful, "even a bit sleepy." She was well received by her husband's family and was further reassured by the various joyful reunions taking place around her. Her apprehensions were soon erased.

Barbara remembers the efficiency and hospitality of the Immigration staff and volunteers. "The fact that I couldn't converse with them in the English language didn't seem to bother them or even surprise them. As I found out later, this was a common occurrence at Pier 21 during the first half of the 20th century."

Heinz and Erika Prager are immigrants from Germany who have had the unique experience of landing at Pier 21 not once, but on two memorable occasions. They first arrived on a sunny day in April of 1958, intent on settling permanently in Canada. To the consternation of their families in Germany, they had decided three months earlier to leave their old homeland in search of a new life.

"You may go," Erika's father had reluctantly conceded, "but you must take with you enough money for the return fare in case you don't like it there." As did the families of so many other European emigrants of that time, Erika's parents thought they would never see their daughter again.

Erika's mother also advised her daughter to ask for "the German Sister" if she needed help upon arrival. Although Erika never did press upon Sister Kelly for help, the linguistic talents of "the German Sister" were in constant demand at Pier 21.

Heinz and Erika arrived with a large group of immigrants from Germany, Holland, and Italy. Cradling their eleven-month-old son, Udo, the young couple was ushered into the Pier 21 reception hall, where they waited for several hours before being summoned forth with their documents.

Finally, they were on their way out of the Pier where they were met by a brother-in-law who had been living in Eastern Passage. Erika remembers the drive across the Angus L. Macdonald Bridge, and her impression of the journey to Eastern Passage, "I thought I had come to the end of the world! I was used to tall buildings and big churches, and then I saw all the little wooden houses here . . ."

With no English and no orientation to the area, life in Eastern Passage was difficult. Although Heinz readily found work as a bricklayer, living with their brother-in-law and his large family proved arduous and left the Pragers feeling sad, isolated, and lost. Reluctantly, they began to realize that they had been blatantly mislead by their relatives who had painted such a glowing but unrealistic picture of life in Canada. The relationship between the families grew more strained and threatened to disintegrate altogether.

Things began to improve finally, when the Pragers were able to obtain an apartment of their own. But an insidious bout of homesickness continued to haunt them and eventually drove them back to Germany in 1962, this time with two sons in tow. However, Germany too had changed and even their beloved families and friends seemed different somehow, irrevocably altered by time. Within a month of their arrival the Pragers made the decision to embark on one final voyage on the high seas, this time on route to a permanent home in Canada.

On a cold, foggy spring day in 1963, the Pragers sailed once again into Halifax harbour. They were happy to be back; this time they knew they had come home to stay. Almost as a form of unpretentious welcome, an immigration guard for whom Heinz had earlier built a fireplace greeted him casually, "Hello Heinz, where've you been?"

Shortly thereafter, Heinz resumed work with his former employer and the couple started building a home in Dartmouth, Nova Scotia. There they remain today, happily settled, the urge to roam long since vanished. Concludes Erika who has returned to Germany to visit her family on a number

A farewell party aboard the S.S. *Maasdam* as she lay anchored just outside of the Halifax Harbour, April 1958. On the right are Heinz and Erika Prager with their son Udo in the highchair.

Courtesy - Heinz and Erika Prager

of occasions, "I wouldn't go back to live in Germany or anywhere else."

In the late 1950s Hungary experienced a bloody rebellion that resulted in a mass exodus of its people. To foreign shores they fled, leaving behind a beloved country no longer recognizable to them. Meanwhile, preparations were being made in Canada and in Halifax to receive a large number of the Hungarian refugees.

The Rockhead Quarantine Hospital, the larger of the two buildings, was again pressed into service as a facility for the detention and accommodation of the hundreds of refugees expected. With Inspector E. Munro appointed as Officer-in-Charge, a full complement of immigration staff was assigned to duty at Rockhead. Caterers and waitresses, and guards and matrons alike converged upon the hospital and prepared for the arrival of the Hungarians.

Upon completion of extensive renovations, Rockhead stood ready to receive 550 people. Here the refugees would be detained until they had been medically cleared by the "immigration doctors," physicians employed with the Department of National Health and Welfare. Finally, all was ready.

Mere days later, the first group of 120 refugees arrived on the Cunard liner, **Ivernia**. Next to arrive was the **Carinthia**, followed by the **Cascania**, the **Castel Biano**, and others. When the exodus out of Hungary had finally subsided, an estimated 35,000 Hungarian refugees had been received by Canada. Approximately half arrived by way of Pier 21.

At Rockhead, provisions had been made enabling families to be accommodated as a unit. Single men and single women would be housed in separate sections of the building. In trying to enforce these procedures, one immigration officer experienced unexpected difficulty with one of the detainees, a young boy who insisted on being admitted to the women's quarters. Only when an interpreter appeared on the scene was the situation resolved: the young boy was actually a young girl who had cropped her hair and donned her brother's clothing as part of her effort to escape Hungary.

Stew Grant, then on staff with Immigration at Pier 21,

**A Displaced Persons party in May 1949 at Pier 21,
Rockhead Quarantine Hospital.**

remembers that when the first group of refugees converged upon Rockhead, the new chef stationed there was uncertain about what he should prepare for them. With a well-stocked larder that included one hundred dozen eggs, he decided on a breakfast menu that would include generous portions of fried and scrambled eggs. The eggs were met with such enthusiasm that the chef was heard to say hours later, "I can't get them to stop eating!"

There were among the refugees at Rockhead, those who were unable to meet the medical requirements for entry into Canada. These unfortunates had contracted tuberculosis and their deportation seemed imminent. Yet, even as they mired in the depths of their own despair, public sympathy for their plight was gaining momentum.

Then, in September of 1959, coincidentally decreed as the Year of the Refugee by the United Nations, Canada changed its medical requirements for the Hungarian refugees. Those who formerly risked deportation due to illness would now be allowed to stay. Canada went one important step further in its humanitarian approach: it announced that the cost for the treatment of refugees with tuberculosis would be assumed by the government. By the end of that year, the Minister of External Affairs estimated that, as a result of these actions by the government, at least one hundred families with members afflicted with tuberculosis had been allowed entry into Canada.

Dr. L.R. Hirtle was one of the "Immigration Doctors" who cared for the tuberculosis patients in the smaller hospital. Dr. Hirtle remembers that in general, many of the refugees were sickly upon arrival and in need of medical attention. The children were often the ones who carried the infectious diseases.

One Hungarian refugee with graphic and sometimes painful memories of his first year in Canada is Joseph Vermes of Halifax. Joseph and his wife and infant son had been living in a DP camp in Ireland, when, in 1958, they were selected to be part of a group of 150 refugees slated for travel to Canada. Joseph, then twenty-six years old, vividly remembers their October arrival in Saint John, New Brunswick: they had been transported on an army plane that had lost the use of two engines during the flight. "I could see sparks and flames coming from the engines before they were shut off," he said, shuddering at the recollection. "We were very frightened, we thought we were going to die."

Joseph had been trained as an electrician technician in his native Hungary and was eager to ply his trade in Canada. Yet, because he spoke no English, he was unable to write his trade examinations and therefore unable to work in his area of expertise. Frustrated, but doggedly determined, he took a job in a lumberyard. It was winter and although he had no winter clothing, he worked outdoors, carrying and stacking lumber. His first day on the job completed, his hands were a bloodied mass of swollen pulp. A week later he received his first pay-check and purchased a coat, boots, and gloves. The following week he was laid off.

Meanwhile, his pregnant wife had suffered a miscarriage and had been admitted to hospital. Joseph was left caring for his one-year old son, yet all the while on the lookout for work. On his second job, he was the target of blatant racial prejudice, and again he was fired.

"Send me back to Hungary and let me die in honor!" he begged of the Immigration officials, "I am proud, I want to provide for my family, I don't want to be a bum!"

Instead of sending him back to his home country, however, Immigration convinced him to start anew in Nova Scotia. At this point he had been in Canada for seven months.

The Vermes family was ensuingly transported to Pier 21 where they remained for a period of five weeks. During that time Joseph searched unrelentingly for work, walking for miles and completing dozens of application forms. Both he and his wife found life at Pier 21 difficult. "It was like a jail," he remembers. "There were bars there, and an evening curfew. I wanted to provide and just couldn't seem to. I was full of energy and anxious to work. It was a very bad time."

Then suddenly his fortune began to change. A Dutch upholsterer who happened to be picking up some furniture at Pier 21 one day, was asked by one of the Immigration officials, "Do you have any work for this honest Hungarian here?" Joseph was hired at a wage of thirty-five dollars a week, and immediately moved out of Pier 21. He was on his way to independence.

Today Joseph Vermes lives in Dartmouth, Nova Scotia, and owns a successful upholstery company. As well, he teaches a popular upholstery course offered by the continuing education system, and enjoys carving, painting and wine making in the little spare time he has. When the occasion to do so arises, he willingly offers services as an interpreter. Joseph remains grateful to the Immigration person who gave him his first break, and to Canada for the life he has found here.

For Pier 21, the 1950s was a decade of animated activity, an energetic heyday of immigration to Canada. Along with the new arrivals came a rich and colorful mosaic of culture, customs and ethnic particularities.

Many of the immigrants brought with them an interesting assortment of food and foodstuffs that received the vigilant attention of the landing officials. To the consternation of agricultural and customs officers, many of the Italian immigrants came laden with containers of wine, pepperonis, salamis, and cheese of all kinds. At times aromas of undefinable description laced the air in the reception hall.

One day a staff guard was having difficulty directing immigrants to a series of empty seats near a man who sat with a towel on his lap. Through an interpreter, the people voiced their concern about a bad smell that seemed to be emanating from this man. When he was finally coaxed to unfold his towel, a lump of very unfresh octopus flesh was exposed. This "precious cargo" had travelled with him all the way from his home country. The immediate dilemma was resolved when the octopus was taken into temporary custody.

Another delicacy that was judiciously guarded by its owners was a kind of cheese made of goat's milk. It is said to have left a memorable odor wafting in the nostrils of the Pier 21 staff.

Immigration officials also learned to exercise caution in the examination of seemingly benign items such as tins of cooking oil. Many families brought with them a five-litre tin of oil, the lid of which had been carefully soldered to the container. The Pier 21 staff ordinarily paid little attention to the tins. That nonchalance came to an abrupt end one day when a tin was opened at random to reveal a handgun inside. From that point on, all tins were opened and carefully examined. One undesirable side effect of this new procedure was the transformation of the floor in the examination area to a treacherous, well-lubricated oil slick.

Another food item that proved to be a nuisance was one that was distributed to immigrants in the form of free samples. The Kelloggs company began the practise of handing out small boxes of corn flakes to all arrivals. Not recognizing this to be breakfast cereal, many of the recipients sought to dispose of the corn flakes after initial examination. More often than not, the floor of Pier 21 was thickly littered with corn flakes and empty boxes.

A free sample distributed by Imperial Tobacco generated considerably more interest among the arrivals. Ogden's tobacco and cigarette papers were given to the men; the women received Turret cigarettes. Any doubt about the universal appeal of tobacco would have been quickly dissipated at Pier 21; the unexpected luxuries were eagerly welcomed and zealously guarded by the recipients.

Not all of the food brought by immigrants made it across the threshold of Canada and onto the trains. Indeed, the number of confiscations prompted the port veterinarian, Dr. D.M. Harlow, to request in 1958 that he be allotted more space at Pier 21. Apparently, the extra space was needed to house equipment used for the inspection of baggage, to store items for pending fumigation, and to store meat destined for incineration.

Pier 21 was occasionally infested with cockroaches, a problem that was undoubtedly perpetrated by foods being brought by the immigrants. At one point a patented cockroach control system was installed in an attempt to solve the problem. Unfortunately, the effects of the system proved more nauseating than the cockroaches. The system was quickly dismissed and the offending insects were again attacked in the conventional manner.

A variety of food services were available at Pier 21. A full menu was offered in each of the Pier's two large cafeterias, and a canteen from which groceries could be purchased was located in the Annex. The most popular canteen items were bread and butter, cheese, sardines, canned meat, and fruits in season. In the late 1940s, a full-course, cafeteria meal could be had at a cost of fifty-five cents. For the long train journey, a cardboard box "special" was offered by the canteen for two dollars.

LEFT:
Cook Paul Ivy (right) was in charge of the immigration dining room. Circa 1950.

RIGHT:
The immigration canteen in the Customs Annex. Newcomers could purchase light groceries for the train journey inland. Circa 1950.

LEFT:
The entrance to the Immigration Annex, via Terminal Road, 1955.

All photos courtesy - CEIC

Pier 21's reception/waiting area, where immigrants awaited processing. 1950s photo.

The procedure for processing the immigrants remained largely as it had been prior to the war. Passengers were disembarked from the liners in groups of a few hundred, and escorted into the reception hall. At the back of the hall stood a series of large wire cages, remnants of an earlier era perhaps, when not much thought was given to the negative impression that might have been left with the new arrivals. The cages were intended not for forcible confinement, but rather to speed up processing. While the immigrants were being processed, their hand luggage was kept in the cages under lock and key.

Yet, there were those among the Pier's staff who had reservations about the appropriateness of cages at an immigration facility. Bill Marks, now Director of Immi-

The cages in the Pier 21 reception area. These cages were the subject of controversy regarding their appropriateness. Circa 1950.

gration for Nova Scotia, remembers his first day of work at Pier 21. The year was 1954.

"Frankly I was troubled by all the wire cages and the way these docile immigrants were being tagged with different coloured tags and moved from one location to the next," Mr. Marks reflected. "I must also admit the bars on all the windows made me a little uneasy."

Mr. Marks was not the only employee who was disconcerted by the wire enclosures. H.P. Wade, then the Officer-in-Charge of Immigration, also had strong views about their propriety at Pier 21. In February of 1956 and with the support of Immigration Officials in Ottawa, Mr. Wade registered a request with the Port Manager to replace the cages with a counter that would serve as a partition to keep hand baggage organized. When the request was granted a short time later, the cages were removed and the Pier lost much of its unpropitious appearance.

From time to time, singular events at the Pier created a buzz of conversation and a stir of savory excitement. In the mid-1950s, an ocean liner docked in Halifax with its load of passengers, including the body of a Canadian woman, previously landed as an immigrant, who had died suddenly during the voyage. At Pier 21, a routine search of her personal effects produced a sum of cash that is reported to have ranged in the area of one hundred thousand dollars. Startled, immigration officials quickly locked the money in the Pier safe, where it was ordered to remain until further notice.

News of the find spread quickly along the waterfront. The Officer in Charge, Jeff Christie, fearing the possibility of an attempted robbery, quietly deposited the money in a local bank where it remained until the woman's estate had been settled.

An unverified story that is still often repeated tells of the gold bullion, reportedly worth millions of dollars, that was brought in to Halifax by warship during the Second World War. It was said that the gold was stored for some time in the Pier's large, walk-in vault. Even today there is speculation over whatever became of the considerable fortune in gold. The vault at the Pier, meanwhile, has been empty of all but cobwebs for many years.

During the Pier's heyday, the vault was also used to safeguard the patronage list for locally hired employment in the kitchen, and for the suppliers of stationery, groceries, cleaning agents, lightbulbs, etc. This generated much amusement among the Immigration staff, who, as Civil Servants were immune to patronage appointments. Yet, they too had been selected from a list, albeit one that was non-partisan in nature.

Another intriguing event took place in the late 1950s when a Russian defector arrived as a stowaway on an Italian ship. Russian diplomats were quick to arrive on the scene and were fervent in their insistance that they be allowed to interview the defector without Canadian officials present.

**The S.S. *Rotterdam* prepares to disembark its passengers, 1951.
Pier 21's gangway is moving into place.**

Photo by Cooper/Hayes, Halifax
Courtesy - National Harbours Board

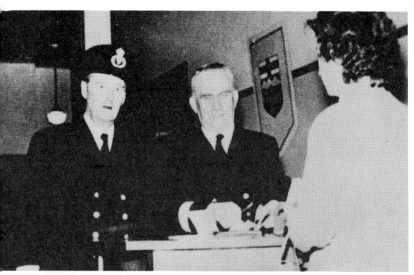

**The first step in processing was a medical inspection.
L-R: Dr. Sullivan, Dr. Harris, and a new immigrant. Photo 1950s.**
Courtesy - CEIC

**New arrivals have their documents examined by Immigration
Officers. 1950s photo.**
Courtesy - CEIC

Canadian officials were equally adamant that they would be present at all meetings with the defector, Petrovich. While the diplomatic battle raged on, Petrovich was housed in the Pier's immigration quarters. His stay lasted for almost twelve months, when word finally came that he would be allowed to remain in Canada.

On a Christmas Eve in the late 1950s, the **Argentina** and the **Vulcania** arrived in Halifax with a combined passenger load numbering eighteen hundred. Not wanting to usher the new arrivals to their waiting trains without offering some semblance of a Christmas feast, the cafeteria and kitchen staff were challenged to prepare a full-course Christmas meal. The kitchen and staff were taxed to the limits, but when the train left several hours later, the passengers had been warmly welcomed to Canada with a traditional Christmas dinner.

Although no statistics are available, records show that the Pier's detention and cell quarters were well used. Yet, the number of people who were detained and eventually deported represents only a minuscule percentage of the vast number who came to stay. One Immigration officer commented that he and his colleagues wielded their authority to deport with careful vigilance. "I could spot an illegal a mile away, anyone of us could. We'd look over the reception area and select those about whom we had an uneasy feeling. These, we'd refer for a more complete examination. While not all were illegals, we caught a few who were."

Having people in detention brought about a number of attempted escapes. In 1948, an inmate managed to escape through the ceiling by climbing over the partitions in the washroom. Also in 1948, a less fortunate detainee bungled his own escape by jumping headfirst into the harbour and suffering a serious head injury. In 1953, a group of three escaped by forcing apart the upright steel bars on the windows.

To the consternation of Security Personnel, there were times when others placed themselves in perilous situations at Pier 21. In the late 1940s, two children made their way to the roof of the building where they hovered dangerously near the edge. On another occasion, a man experiencing mental difficulties climbed onto the roof and began throwing his baggage into the harbour. Perhaps the saddest case of all occurred in the mid 1960s when the body of a ship's deserter was found hanging from the rafters. Although the possibility of murder was considered, it was concluded that suicide had been committed.

By the end of the 1950s, a number of telltale signs hinted loudly that the era of Pier 21 was slowly drawing to a close. The age of the jet liner had arrived, the age of the ocean liner was ineluctably fading into the past. The Pier herself was showing the inevitable signs of advanced age. Yet, her final hour of service had not yet arrived. There remained one more decade in which to play a part, one more decade to serve as the gateway, the front door, to Canada.

The Ending
of an Era

Immigration officials join a ship's captain (left) for a moment of relaxation. 1940 photo.

Courtesy - Canadian Pacific Railway Company

A chapter in the annals of twentieth century history will undoubtedly be reserved to document the era of the magnificent ocean liner, the era when the gap between the continents was effectively bridged with a noble fleet of ultra-modern steamers. Sleek and elegant, the powerful vessels raced their way across the high seas, back and forth, leaving in their wake the graceful undulation of water that has been but momentarily disturbed. Heeding neither the weather nor the season, they uncomplainingly plied the waters of the mighty Atlantic.

Week after week, year after year, the huge ships were towed into the harbour and tied up at Pier 21. Those who strolled regularly on the Halifax waterfront might have feasted their eyes on any of a large number of liners; there were the Queens, **Elizabeth** and **Mary**, always regal visitors to the port. There were the **Mauretania** and the **Maasdam**, the **Athenia** and the **Aquitania**. There were the **Olympic**, the **Anna Salem**, and the **Samaria**. And there were many more. They navigated the oceans on behalf of their owners — among them, Cunard, Furness, White Star, North German Lloyd, Italian Line, CP, CN Steamships, and Anchor Donaldson.

In the mid-1950s, Halifax had the memorable occasion to witness, in a single day, the arrival of five large ocean liners, including the **Queen Elizabeth**. The Port of New York had been rendered inoperative by a longshoremen's strike and ocean traffic had therefore been diverted to Halifax. On that particular day and with the assistance of U.S. Immigration·

authorities, more than 3,800 passengers were processed at Pier 21. The pageantry in the reception hall was perhaps surpassed only by the colorful regatta in the harbour.

This was also the era when a meal aboard ship varied from gourmet fare served on linen-clad tables adorned with silverware and fresh flowers, to a simple snack eaten out of one's own luggage. The Canadian Immigration Officers and staff came to look forward to invitations to dine aboard the visiting ships that lay docked at Pier 21.

Frank Dunham recalls the first time he and a colleague were invited to dine aboard ship. The ship was the elegant **Queen Frederica** and the year was 1967. Frank and his colleague served themselves generously from the heaping platters that were placed before them. To the chagrin of both men, it was only when the steaks were brought out that they realized they had unwittintly filled themselves on fancy hors d'oeuvres. Apparently the more seasoned officers, those who had dined aboard the **Queen Frederica** before and were well aware of her extensive menu, had sat back and watched the two novices in silent amusement.

The birth of a baby while at sea was not an altogether infrequent occurrence and never failed to generate excitement at the port of arrival. In February of 1949, a baby girl was born aboard the **Samaria** and was given the name, Samaria. In late 1950, "Baby Boy Bauer" was added to the manifest of the **Nea Hellas**. In June of 1952, a child was born aboard the **Anna Salem**, of parents destined for Merlin, Ontario. That child too was named after the ship on which she had been born. It is thought, however, that the liner, **Roma**, holds the record for the most births at sea. The boys were frequently named Romano, and the girls were given the name, Roma.

Even the mighty ocean vessel suffered occasionally at the hands of a careless or over-exuberant captain. On July 28, 1960, the USS **Carrier Essex** was preparing to leave its berth at Pier 21. As it swung away, it underestimated the length of its own forward bridge and left a gaping hole in the side of Pier 21. Inside, the damage was limited to the medical quarters, where the startled staff stood in silent astonishment.

Alan Green, QC, of Halifax had decided to take a

detour on his way to work that morning and was witness to the event. He recalls that from where he stood, it was obvious that the American ship did not have enough clearance to manoeuver itself successfully away from the dock. He knew the collision was inevitable, yet could do nothing but watch. As a band played 'Anchors Aweigh,' the bridge of the ship crashed into the groaning Pier. Laughter tittered among the crowd and a Canadian soldier was overhead to say, "Thank God we have the Army!" Understandably, the Royal Canadian Navy was quick to disassociate itself from the incident.

The damage was estimated at five thousand dollars, but the nature of the incident prompted officials of the National Harbours Board (formerly the Halifax Port Commissioners) to hold the U.S. Navy responsible. Meanwhile, the medical staff was temporarily relocated and repair work to the damaged area was begun.

Damage to the Pier inflicted by the US Carrier _Essex_ at 9:10 a.m., July 28, 1960.

Courtesy - Halifax Port Corporation

At around the same time the **Arosa Kulm** and a Cunard liner were racing to the dock, each attempting to be the first to be berthed and offloaded. Arriving first meant avoiding the long wait while the other ship was being serviced. The **Arosa Kulm** won the race but the strain of the contest had taken its toll on the captain; within minutes of pulling away from the dock to return to Germany, he collapsed and suffered a fatal heart attack.

In the early 1960s it was becoming increasingly apparent that the era of the ocean liner was drawing to a close. More and more travellers were beginning to opt for the efficiency and convenience of air travel. The ships that had always been filled to repletion were now arriving half empty. The number of stately liners to call at Halifax began to dwindle and their visits became less and less frequent.

In late 1967 the media announced that the Cunard liner, **Carinthia**, had just paid her last visit to Halifax and that she was being sold upon her return to Southhampton. On this, her last call, she had carried only 240 passengers, a far cry from her usual list of 800. For the **Carinthia** as for so many of the other liners, the inevitable scrap heap marked a sad and ungracious end. Shortly after the **Carinthia**'s farewell stopover, the **Sylvania** and the **Carmania** also paid their last call at Pier 21.

Statistics revealed that in 1968 12,000 passengers had arrived in Nova Scotia by ship while 13,832 had travelled by air. It was by now apparent that the Port of Halifax was in the throes of a dramatic metamorphosis, one that would mark the inevitable demise of a venerable immigration facility.

Ironically, the last large groups of people to be processed at Pier 21 arrived not by ship but by airplane. Between 1961 and 1963 large numbers of Cubans sought refugee status in Gander, Newfoundland, where they had arrived by airplane. They hoped to gain eventual access to the United States. However, because an American visa could take up to six months to procure, the Cubans were transported to Halifax where they were temporarily housed at Pier 21. At one point there were over one hundred Cubans temporarily in residence at the Pier.

Documentation illustrates that the resourceful Cubans wasted no time settling into their new situation:

> Coming from all walks of life, from land-owners to doctors and from aircraft pilots to farmers, the refugees set up their own committees and appointed spokesmen to deal with the everyday problems of adjusting to strange surroundings and a new culture. Language training of a basic sort was begun, and negotiations (were) carried out on everything from the provision of a bed and board for a refugee with back trouble to the preparation of an all-Cuban meal in the Pier kitchen. To the bemusement of Immigration staff, the two spokesmen in such everyday negotiations were a criminal lawyer and a commercial lawyer, both very adept at achieving their ends.[57]

From time to time the Cubans took over the Pier kitchen to prepare their own special treats, one of which was salt cod. The fish was served with chopped onion, hard boiled eggs, and an egg sauce.

On another occasion, an on-duty guard at the Pier answered the telephone only to be informed that he had just won twenty-five dollars in a random-dial contest. The guard accepted the cheque and took two of the Cuban women to the nearest supermarket. It was difficult for the enthusiastic shoppers to make a selection and to keep the purchases limited to the amount of the prize. Finally, cake and ice cream, the ultimate and universal treat for children, was decided upon and carried back to the Pier.

While waiting for their American visas, some of the Cubans were compelled to spend Christmas at Pier 21. Had it not been for the staff and several volunteers, the holiday season could have been a drab and ardous time. Instead, considerable effort was made to ensure that the Cuban children enjoyed their traditional Christmas celebration.

In "Room 33" an altar was lovingly created, using a white tablecloth borrowed from the kitchen. A memorable party, complete with Christmas dinner, donated gifts, and a decorated tree, was organized for the group which included twenty-four wives and fourteen children. Even Santa Claus went to unusual lengths to prepare himself to greet the Cuban children — it was decided that the jolly old man would be played by one of the refugees so that he would be easily understood by the little ones.

After the departure of the Cubans, the Pier 21 detention quarters remained largely empty. Although travellers continued to arrive sporadically, the largest groups coming from Italy and Greece, the Pier's lofty reception hall had acquired a hollow, ominous echo.

In the latter part of the 1960s, groups of Czechoslovakian refugees were housed at Pier 21, pending the location of suitable accommodations elsewhere in the city. Very shortly after the arrival of one such group, Father J.R. Brown, the Roman Catholic Port Chaplain, paid them a visit at Pier 21 and asked if there was anything he could do for them.

Father Brown remembers that, "the first couple that came were all smiles, and holding out papers in their hands. As my interpreter listened to them, he started smiling as well. It turned out that the papers were wedding invitations; the couple had planned to be married in Prague the morning of the Russian invasion, and that was still the first thing on their minds."[57]

By the time of the wedding, a dress and veil and all other necessary items had been borrowed from a variety of sources. "One Halifax couple very kindly hosted a reception and another provided a honeymoon," Father Brown recalls. For the young couple, the wedding became a memorable occasion that was witnessed by all of the Czechoslovakian refugees.

Throughout the 1960s the aging Pier continued to be upgraded, perhaps as a tangible protest to her inevitable retirement. In 1961 a water sprinkler system was installed at a cost of $24,800. In the mid 1960s the removal of the bars on the windows was finally authorized by William Stewart, Director General. Stewart himself had arrived at the Pier as an immigrant four decades earlier. He had stared uncomprehendingly at the barred windows and experienced a disquietitude that even now continued to affect him deeply. Bars, he ascertained, were no way to welcome a people to their chosen country.

Subsequently, acetylene torches were brought in and quick work was made of the bars that had served for so long as a dubious welcome at the gateway to Canada.

By the end of the decade, The Department of Manpower and Immigration could no longer justify the continued outlay of considerable monies on a facility that was simply no longer needed. Ocean traffic had all but ceased, and the processing of immigrants had been radically decentralized and deferred to the more than thirty Immigration Centres that were being established at the international airports across Canada.

For the people of Pier 21, this was a most difficult time. Many had spent all of their working years on the waterfront; most had difficulty imagining another job that would fill the void that was now being so keenly experienced. In "The Pier 21 Story," a 1978 publication by Employment and Immigration Canada, the people of the Pier attempted to describe their loss:

> . . . with the closing of Pier 21 a chapter of Canadian life was finished. Gone, apparently forever, was the excitement, the challenge, the exhilaration, of dealing with hundreds or even thousands of immigrants at once — people who had travelled for a week or more to each Canada and who still had a train journey of days before them; people receiving their first impression of a vast, new country; people with special needs and unique problems; people who at Pier 21 were for almost fifty years met, examined, fed, nursed, sometimes housed, assisted with loans, married, even occasionally buried. Pier 21 was in many ways a bustling self-sufficient village hidden within the vast anonymous looking transit shed and the people who worked there will never forget it.[57]

And so, in March of 1971, Pier 21 was quietly closed. It still stands today, its upper floor largely empty, its corridors forever stripped of the endless parade of clip-clipping feet, its reception hall suspended in a perpetual roar of silence.

Gone forever is the era when the Port of Halifax was

used firstly by people — the passengers, merchants, and endless number of suppliers who contributed to the operation of transporting people from place to place. Gone as well is the time when local citizens strolled routinely down to the waterfront to watch the graceful liners dock, to wave their welcome to the many new arrivals on board, and to have their greetings acknowledged with eager eyes and shy, hesitant smiles.

As this colourful and dynamic chapter of Canadian history slips quietly into the past, Halifax's Pier 21 can be proud of the gracious and humanitarian role that she has played in the building of modern-day Canada.

Epilogue

Today the Pier 21 Transit Shed sits as an empty, aging structure, its colorless facade offering little hint of the drama that was once unfolded there. Who, by staring at the ordinary architecture, would conclude that this building had played host to hundreds of thousands of new Canadians? Who would guess that these inauspicious surroundings had received a venerable list of well-known individuals — the royalty of Britain on more than one occasion, Sir Winston Churchill, who to the chagrin of security guards chose to walk the distance from the Pier to the train station, film stars, war heroes, and a long line of political figures? Lamentably, the artless structure itself is powerless to divulge the secrets of its animated past.

From its vantage point on prime waterfront property, Pier 21 gazes out stoically at the passing harbour traffic that no longer knocks upon its door. The passenger liners and freighters have been replaced with gigantic container ships that dutifully plough their way to the container terminals located nearby. The many pleasure boats whisk by, cheerfully oblivious to the low, flat-roofed building where majestic ocean vessels once competed for berthing space.

Over the last fifteen years the lower floor of Pier 21 has continued to serve as a shipping warehouse. The upper floor has seen various tenants come and go. In short, the Pier's vast immigration facility has been without a mandate, its future suspended in a clouded and precarious state of oblivion. In order to survive on its salient waterfront location, Pier 21 will

167

Today, Pier 21's ground floor remains in use as a shipping warehouse. Its top floor remains largely vacant.

Photo - CEIC

need an enduring purpose to carry it solidly into the next century.

Essentially, however, it can be effectively reasoned that, by the very nature of her part in the shaping of Canada, the Pier has inherently been commissioned with a purpose of the utmost importance — that of preserving an integral part of Canadian heritage. Fortunately, there are efforts in place to encourage an impetus in that direction.

The Ottawa-based, Parks Canada Federal Heritage Buildings Review Committee has in its mandate the task to identify, conserve, and manage Canada's heritage properties. The following declaration was recorded in a June, 1984 meeting:

> The peopling of Canada through immigration is a theme of great national significance which should be the subject of major commemoration. Since it is apparent that the complexity of this theme cannot be dealt with adequately at a single site, the Branch should investigate sites with appropriate concentration of surviving resources to interpret it, having regard for both historical periods and geographic distribution.[29]

Few would argue that Pier 21 does not merit recognition as a key immigration historical site. Fewer still would dispute the need to have a lasting, tangible commemoration of the unique era of history that saw the peopling of an entire nation. There are stories, photographs, artifacts and memorabilia to document this era, items that have not yet been lost to the dust of time gone by. A number of exciting options for the documentation of immigration history still exist, but these options too, are rapidly fading.

One option that in recent months has been the subject of much discussion, is the development of an Immigration Museum at the very site where so many Canadians first felt Canadian ground under their feet. A museum at Pier 21 would be easily accessible from city streets as well as from the harbour. A museum within the walls of the immigration centre would serve to capture the very spirit of the immigrant and of the refugee; it would invite the visitor to understand and experience the motives behind the immigrant's decision to leave everything behind in the quest for something new and uncertain. In essence, an immigration museum would stand as an enduring reminder of Canada's social and economic foundation. Such is the potential of Pier 21, a historical facility that could well become one of Canada's most significant museums.

The Multicultural Association of Nova Scotia has for some time been advocating the development of a Multicultural Plaza at Pier 21. Barbara Campbell, Executive Director, has visions of incorporating the museum concept with a commercial enterprise that would contain business offices, boutiques and a centre for the performing arts. She feels strongly that, "Pier 21 is one of Canada's great monuments which must be preserved for future generations."

As well, the complex could contain fine eateries and a visitors' information centre. With a series of balconies, atriums, skylights, and interconnecting walkways, the Pier 21 Transit Shed would have the potential to evolve into one of the most animated and dynamic properties on the Halifax waterfront.

The magnificent seawall at Pier 21 is the ideal berth for the many cruise ships that are beginning to frequent the Halifax harbour. Currently, the ships have but makeshift docking facilities and the passengers have little access to the heart of the city. The Pier 21 seawall combined with a Pier 21 Plaza would provide the type of facility that would serve to attract and welcome the ocean voyagers. Pier 21 was constructed specifically to receive passengers of ocean vessels; it is appropriate that this mandate be bestowed upon her again.

Halifax's Pier 21 is gradually becoming the object of renewed interest, both in the historical sense and in the sense that a new purpose be developed for the venerable Shed. On March 8, 1988 a commemorative ceremony was held on site to mark the sixtieth anniversary of the opening of the Pier. The landing of the immigrants was re-enacted and an impromptu tour of the building sparked considerable interest. The 1988 Nova Scotia Tattoo also leaned heavily on the immigration theme, citing several references to the unpretentious Transit Shed.

As a society grows and develops, it invariably becomes interested in looking over its shoulder to study the path upon which it has travelled. People are inherently interested in their beginnings, in knowing and understanding their origins, in comprehending the metamorphosis that has guided them through the many intricate stages of development to their present-day conformation. For the majority of Canadians, to look over one's shoulder is to see a long, protracted line of immigrants labouring toward Canadian soil. To behold these immigrants is to acknowledge their role in the building of a nation. And to acknowledge their essential part in the making of history is ultimately and irrefutably to recognize the national treasure that is Pier 21.

Appendix A
A Brief History of the Evolution of Canada's Immigration Policy

To examine the history of Canada is to examine its vast and extensive immigration movement. From the time the ancestors of the Native Peoples migrated across the Bering Strait from Asia many centuries ago, to the refugees who arrived in the 1980s, Canada's development as a nation has been molded and catalyzed by the millions of newcomers who have made this country their home.

In 1871 Canada's total population was estimated at 3.6 million. During the next 100 years, 9.3 million people immigrated to Canada. Although some of these newcomers eventually returned to their homelands and many others continued on to the United States, Canada's population in 1971 had nonetheless grown to 21.5 million.

Prior to confederation, the greeting and handling of immigrants had been the responsibility of the various colonial governments. With the first Canada Immigration Act of 1869, immigration became a federal jurisdiction.

Historically, Canada's immigration policy has not been without its darker moments. In 1885 a head tax was imposed on Chinese immigrants, thereby severely curtailing their migration to Canada. In the early 1900s, a group of blacks hoping to immigrate to Alberta from the United States were pointedly warned that they should not waste time and money seeking entry into Canada.

During this time as well, Jews arriving in Halifax were not the recipients of favorable comments. A 1901 report to Ottawa stated that "without a doubt, the Jews were the dirtiest class of immigrants arriving in Halifax." The report went on to describe how the bedding they used while at the immigration facility was alive with vermin. In reply, Ottawa briskly authorized the purchase of straw and a few dozen bed ticks and ordered that they be accommodated "downstairs," in the baggage area.

The manner in which the Jewish arrivals were handled is revealing perhaps, not so much of a country's lack of goodwill, but rather, of Canada's failure to recognize the sheer destitution of a people who were arriving on her doorstep. People by nature are not "dirty"; it is their destitute condition that renders them so.

In 1913 Halifax began the practise of segregating the British arrivals from all other immigrants. After all, noted one Dominion Immigration Agent, it was hardly fair to expect the British immigrants to use the same closets used by the foreigners.

The Canadian Encyclopedia aptly describes the climate of Canada's immigration policy of that time:

> Otherwise immigration policy was concerned mainly with quarantine stations, the responsibilities of transportation companies and the exclusion of criminals, paupers, the diseased and the destitute. But after the massive immigration between 1903 and 1913, WWI and subsequent political upheavals and economic problems, a much more restrictive 'white Canada' immigration policy was implemented and remained unchanged until 1962, when Canada's present universal and nondiscriminatory policy was introduced.[24]

Immigration to Canada peaked in 1913 when 400,870 immigrants were landed on Canadian soil. There were at this time many signs of increasing sentiment by government and the private sector that Canada should remain a predominantely white and Protestant society. To that end, a list of ideal immigrants, in order of descending preference, was established. At the top of the list were the British and white Americans. Next came the French, Belgians, Dutch, Scandinavians, Swiss, Finns, Russians, Austro-Hungarians,

Germans, Ukrainians and Poles. Near the bottom of the list were those the government deemed less assimilable: the Italians, South Slavs, Greeks and Syrians. At the very bottom were the Jews, Asians, and blacks.

During the war years, Canada's notoriety as a country that closed its doors to the Jewish victims of Nazi Germany was well established. Yet, in the period following World War II, Canada was one of the first countries to open its doors to the thousands of refugees and Displaced Persons from Eastern and Southern Europe.

Since the time of the Second World War, government departments responsible for immigration have been regrouped three times — the Department of Citizenship and Immigration (1950-1965), the Department of Manpower and Immigration (1966-1977), and currently, the Canada Employment and Immigration Commission. Prior to the establishments of these departments, the immigration portfolio had been under the jurisdiction of various federal departments, among them Agriculture, the Department of the Interior, and Mines and Resources.

In the 1970s a Green Paper on Immigration Policy was prepared, much of which was absorbed into the 1978 Immigration Act. For the first time a set of immigration objectives was established, including a commitment to non-discrimination and to the country's international obligations towards refugees.

Over the years Canada's immigration policy has matured to one that appeals to the fair-minded and the compassionate. A unique feature of the policy is the provision that enables any individual wishing to remain in Canada to take his case directly to the Minister for consideration.

But the metamorphosis of this policy has not taken place without difficulty; through the decades and generations it has been subjected to the influences of the time. In the same way, it has served to mirror the changes experienced by a society struggling to assume an identity of its own.

Today Canada is recognized as a bastion of democracy, a society that supports the individual and human rights of its peoples. And today this philosophy is inherently reflected in Canada's immigration policies and programs.

Appendix B
Immigration through Halifax
Prior to 1928

A seafarer arriving at the Port of Halifax in the nineteenth century would have been grateful for the sight of land after a long, perilous sojourn at sea. As his fragile craft slipped into the harbour he would have noted the dark rugged coastline, haphazardly dotted with small, wooden structures. On his right he would have observed the waves of his wake quietly lapping the shores of a series of islands — Sambro, McNabs, Devil's, and George's. On his left, the lush forest of Point Pleasant would have appeared to be growing right up to the edge of the beach. Directly before him he would have gazed reverently at the magnificent Citadel Hill rising up from behind a collection of sheds that littered the waterfront.

So this was Halifax! This was the city with the perfect harbour, deep, sheltered, and ice free. This was the front door of a country that, while roughly hewn and still in its infancy, was nonetheless steadily drawing its population from the excesses of Europe.

They came like iron filings to the magnet, lured by the prospects of a new beginning and a better life. They endured the perils of the sea, the hardships of a sixteen-week voyage in an open, leaking vessel, the starvation that followed when the pitifully inadequate rations inevitably ran out. Many perished under the most tragic of circumstances.

The Acadian Recorder made the disturbing comment in July, 1839, that, "Upon the whole we conscientiously believe that one-fourth of all immigrants who sail . . . never reach America." *The Recorder* went as far as to add that many of the vessels used in the transport of immigrants across the Atlantic were fit only for firewood.

The April 23, 1849 edition of the *Novascotian* reported the astounding fact that no less than 20,000 immigrants had perished of ship fever at sea or in the various hospitals in North American ports.

During this era of wooden ships and sails, many vessels ran into trouble off Sable Island, ominously dubbed the "Graveyard of the Atlantic." In April of 1873, 562 people perished when the **Atlantic** ran aground on the rocks off Prospect, just a few miles from the Port of Halifax. And in 1883 a German vessel, so close to her Halifax destination, was wrecked just outside of the harbour with a loss of sixteen lives.

With the first Canada Immigration Act of 1869, Halifax had been established as one of eight Canadian locations where immigrants would be received and "processed." When Halifax had been further granted the status of Port of Entry in 1881, its recognition as a destination for countless numbers of immigrants had been assured.

By 1881 the sailing ships had been largely replaced by the mighty steamers. This dramatically changed the immigration scene on the Halifax Waterfront; ocean crossings which had previously taken up to three months to complete were now reduced to a period of twelve to sixteen days, thereby ensuring that passengers were generally in better health upon arrival. As well, passenger traffic increased as ocean liners steamed across the Atlantic in a fraction of the time it would have taken their predecessors to complete the journey.

By the early 1900s it was common to see the majestic Allan liners docked in Halifax — the **Tunisian**, the **Sarmantian**, the **Corthaginian**, and the **Mongolian**. A 1905 report estimated that more than 18,000 passengers had arrived in Halifax in the previous six-month period.

As a group, the early arrivals seem to have been a cut above the stereotypical penniless, friendless souls who arrived in Canada with nothing but dim prospects. Immigration reports of that time frequently contained favorable comments about the calibre of the new arrivals. In an 1888 report, one official wrote, "The class of people landing here has been an excellent one, very few poor immigrants have arrived and I have found none to be placed on the list of Paupers." It was estimated at the time that the average value of cash and effects brought by each immigrant was in the vicinity of fifty dollars.

The immigrant pauper was not a common sight on the Halifax waterfront. A plausible explanation for this relative rarity lay in an 1880 Order-in-Council which prohibited paupers from gaining entry into Canada. Any pauper who did manage to come as far as Halifax was quickly detected and swiftly ushered aboard the ship upon which he had arrived, to be delivered back to his country of origin at the expense of the transportation company.

The mood of the time is further reflected in a front page article of an 1899 issue of *The Halifax Herald*. It reads in part:

> That Canada should retain the good character she has gained is an economic question of permanent interest, a problem of practical politics that affects every one of her children. This nation is now in course of construction and the future will depend largely upon the elements out of which its population is composed.[61]

A great many of the immigrants at that time were British subjects from the United Kingdom. Because of Canada's former status as a British colony and because Canadians were British subjects as well, these immigrants were not looked upon as foreigners, but rather, were entitled to preferential treatment. Upon arrival they were billeted in separate quarters and identified as English, a recognition that undoubtedly worked greatly to their advantage.

One persistent problem among the early immigrants involved the excesses of alcohol. In an 1883 report immigration officials complained about the alarming prevalence of alcohol among certain groups of arrivals. Invariably, there are accounts of alcohol related mishaps: one inebriated immigrant was reported to have fallen from a train as it was pulling out of the station. His foot was partially severed.

Another concern of the time was with the number of single women arriving, seemingly without purpose and destination. Some had been coerced aboard ship at the point of departure, others arrived ready to resume their dubious trade in a new country. An immigration official had this to say in a 1902 report:

> I would mention the fact that considerable difficulty has been experienced with girls sent out to this country by parties on the other side who have hoped in the change of locality to better their condition in more ways than one. The experiment has met with very poor success . . . [2]

Many of these unfortunates arrived in a state of poor health and pitiful hygiene. One matron employed with Immigration is said to have requested rubber gloves to be used in the handling of these destitute women. A large number was eventually deported.

Another group of would-be immigrants was comprised of the seamen who deserted their foreign ships while berthed at Halifax. Many of them had been shanghaied at the port of departure and took advantage of the earliest opportunity to desert ship in Halifax. It has been said that the practice of shanghaiing went on in Halifax also, often in arrangement with boarding house owners who preyed upon their unsuspecting tenants.

The arrivals in 1899 of the **Lake Huron** and the **Lake Superior,** each with 2,000 Doukhobors on board, stirred a considerable amount of interest in Halifax. The Doukhobors were a fine example of the type of citizen Canada was looking for. They were a strong people, able agriculturists, and eager to start anew. One newspaper reported enthusiastically that they "excited the imagination of all. They are a fine looking lot of people, with honest faces and stalwart frames." They would contribute greatly to the settlement of western Canada, a priority with the Canadian government of that time.

Among the most interesting categories of immigrants to come to Halifax were children from the orphanages and slums of England. Special non-government, benevolent agencies were organized for this purpose and established in England as well as in Canada. In England these agencies were responsible for gathering the children, screening them, and preparing them for immigration.

It is estimated that some 95,000 children and juveniles arrived under this form of private sponsorship between 1883 and 1930. Of this number, 5,000 were eventually settled in the Maritime provinces.

Upon their arrival in Halifax the children were temporarily housed in receiving homes, two of which were the Stirling home in Aylesford and the Middlemore Home in Halifax. From there they were sent to live with the sponsoring families. Most of the boys were placed in farm homes while the girls were employed in domestic situations in both urban and rural settings.

The agencies of placement continued to remain responsible for the children until they had reached nineteen years of age. As well, immigration authorities, although not directly involved, maintained an ongoing interest and occasionally visited various immigrant children to check on their situation.

During these early years the Halifax waterfront was alive with the hustle and bustle of people on the move. In the shadow of the great ocean liners, a never-ending queue of newcomers wended its way from the dock to the immigration facility. Every day of the year they arrived, regardless of the weather or season. Amidst the heaps of luggage strewn upon the dock, families in ragged cloth coats huddled together in a vain attempt to ward off the bitter winter cold. And in the heat of summer they landed, the ever-present, uniformed immigration personnel busily milling around them.

The war years served to slow the tide of immigration but Halifax remained a busy place with the continuous presence of the military. In the years immediately following the war to end all wars, the immigration tap was again turned on as Canada made plans to receive the war victims from continental and eastern Europe. At first they came in a trickle, then in a steady stream, all with the same hollowed look of despair in their eyes. But they were a fiesty lot who carried a precious spark of hope in their hearts. It was this spark that landed them in Halifax, in an alien country, among strangers, alone. It was this spark that spurred them on in the greatest adventure of their lives, that caused them to gamble a dubious past for an uncertain future. Such were the folk who presented themselves as frank candidates for Canadian citizenship in Halifax in the early twentieth century.

It is thought that the first immigration facility in Halifax was located at 40 Bedford Row. The structure was known as the Dominion Building and still stands today, diagonally across from Province House in downtown Halifax. The letterhead on an 1869 report by Dr. Edwin C. Clay, first Dominion Immigration Agent in Halifax, supports this premise; it lists the Department's address as being 40 Bedford Row.

An 1882 report by Dr. Clay mentions the completion of an immigration facility at the Deep Water Terminus, located at the foot of Cogswell Street. Although this new building boasted all of the modern amenities, it rapidly grew too small to handle the increased immigrant traffic. An 1893 inspection report voiced a number of concerns:

> . . . baggage completely fills up space reserved for people; wait for hours wherever standing room can be found, baggage sorted, examined, fumigated and checked. There were it is true a few benches near the stoves but in a crowd they are a small advantage and are particularly unavailable to women and children.
>
> In addition to the discomforts of standing for hours, these people are exposed to cold draughts owing to the necessity of keeping the large door open while the work of fumigating and cooling baggage goes on.
>
> A number of the passengers avail themselves of the meals furnished by the caterer. The majority of the steerage passengers, however, have their own provisions but no place where they can sit comfortably.
>
> Under the present conditions the public can enter the immigration area from many means and mingle and take advantage of the migrants.[35]

In February, 1895, a fire claimed the entire Deep Water Terminus, including the immigration facilities, at an estimated loss of $250,000. Swiftly the immigration officials moved their operation into temporary quarters at the Richmond Railway Station, located at the foot of North Street. Inexplicably, a second fire claimed this facility a mere three months later.

Frustrated, immigration officials sought an Order-in-Council authorizing the construction of a new immigration building on the site of the original Deep Water Terminus. This was granted in November, 1895. The cost of the building, specifically for immigration, was not to exceed $30,000.

The new single-storey facility, to be known as Pier 2, was opened in 1897 and was touted as one of the best immigration reception buildings in North America. Before long, however, Pier 2 as well became the object of many complaints, the chief one being the problem of overcrowding. Plans were made to add a second storey; this was completed in 1915.

By this time it had become obvious that, despite the newly completed expansion, Pier 2 did not have the capacity to handle the ever-increasing ocean traffic that was arriving at its doors. Consequently, a blueprint was drawn up for a large, two-storey facility to be situated in the south end of Halifax.

This structure, to be known to the world as Pier 21, was to be one of the most modern buildings of its time. It was to form part of a new complex in the south end of Halifax that would eventually include a large CNR railway station and the Hotel Nova Scotian, a first-class respite for travellers.

Following the move by Immigration to Pier 21 in 1928, the immigration facility at Pier 2 was turned into a shipping warehouse. In 1933 Pier 2 and its contents were entirely destroyed in a devastating fire that smoldered insidiously for several days. When the last stubborn embers had finally been extinguished, the loss of building and considerable contents was estimated at two million dollars.

Contributors

(Personal Correspondence or Interview)

N. Akerlund
Brenda Bennett
Mary Bowser
Ian Cameron
Barbara Campbell
D. Owen Carrigan
Felice Catalano
Fenton C. Crosman
Robert Deitz
Màbel Doherty
Frank Dunham
Marianne Ferguson
Stewart Grant
Alan Green
L.R. Hirtle
Florence Kelly

Maisie Lugar
F.R. MacKinnon
Urban J. Mackinnon
Anna Maloney
William Martin
Clare McDade
Chris Nolan
Erika Prager
Heinz Prager
Gordon Thomas
Alison Trapnell
Konstant Trus
Marguerite Turner
Joseph Vermes
Joy Wilson
Sara Yablon

References

1. Ahern, John E. Letter to W.J.F. Pratt. Halifax: January 8, 1948.

2. Annand, T.W. Report of the Halifax Agent. Halifax: July 1, 1902. Sessional Papers 1903; 25:45.

3. Annand, T.W. Letter to Frank Pedley. Halifax: January 17, 1901.

4. Annual report. Halifax: Halifax Harbour Commissioners. 1933. p. 6.

5. Archbishop Lauds Sisters of Service in Halifax. The Catholic Register. Toronto: The Canadian Register. 1988; August 17.

6. Bennet, C.S. Memo to Port Manager. Halifax: April 14, 1944.

7. Borrett, W.C. *East Coast Port.* Halifax: The Imperial Publishing Co. Ltd. 1944.

8. Borrett, W.C. *Tales Told Under the Old Town Clock.* Halifax: The Imperial Publishing Co. Ltd. 1945.

9. C.N.R. Halifax Ocean Terminals. Proposed Immigration Facilities. Sheds No. 21 & 22 — General Layout. Moncton: October 31, 1928.

10. Cameron, Ian. The Quarantine Station on Lawlor's Island 1866-1938. Halifax: Nova Scotia Medical Bulletin 1983; 62:83-87.

11. Cameron, Ian. Halifax and the Cholera Epidemic of 1866. Halifax: Nova Scotia Medical Bulletin 1984; 63:149-153.

12. Cameron, Ian. HMS Pyramus Frigate, Receiving Ship, Hospital. Halifax: Nova Scotia Medical Bulletin 1987; 66:118-120.

13. Cameron, Ian. Camp Hill and the Smallpox Outbreak of 1938. Halifax: Nova Scotia Medical Journal 1988; 67:100-103.

14. Campbell, Barbara. Personal Correspondence. Halifax: July 1988.

15. Carrigan, D. Owen. The Immigrant Experience in Halifax 1881-1931. Halifax: Unpublished. 1986.

16. Chisholm, Michael M. Promoting the Scottish Heritage. Halifax: *The Novascotian*; November 29, 1986.

17. City of Flint Due Here This Morning. *The Halifax Herald*. Halifax: 1939; 64 (219):12.

18. Collins, Doug. *Immigration and the Destruction of Canada*. Richmond Hill: BMG Publishing Ltd. Circa 1970.

19. Collins, Louis W. *In Halifax Town*. Halifax: Privately printed in 1975.

20. Corbett, David C. *Canada's Immigration Policy*. Toronto: University of Toronto Press. 1957.

21. Crosman, Fenton C. Ottawa: Unpublished Notes. 1937.

22. DesLauriers, Rev. Anthony. Halifax: Unpublished Essay. 1963.

23. Dietz, Robert. "Robert Dietz Remembers" in Christmas Past. Halifax: *The Southender* 1984; 1(8):2-14.

24. Dirks, Gerald E. Immigration Policy. *The Canadian Encyclopedia.* Edmonton: Hurtig Publishers 1985; 2:864-866.

25. Doukhobors Have Sailed. *The Halifax Herald.* Halifax: 1899; XXV (42).

26. Duivenvoorden Mitic, Trudy. Halifax's Pier 21 . . . A Gateway to Canada. Halifax: *The Novascotian.* 1986; 5(1):7-9.

27. Duivenvoorden Mitic, Trudy. Spokesman for Immigrants. Halifax: *The Novascotian.* 1987; 6(12): 4-5.

28. Duivenvoorden Mitic, Trudy. A Tradition of Service. Halifax: *The Novascotian* (In Press).

29. Extract from Minutes of Meeting. Federal Heritage Buildings Review Committee. Ottawa: Parks Canada. 1984; June.

30. Haff, Rhoda. America's Immigrants. New York; Henry Z. Walch Inc.

31. Hanington, Brian J. Every Popish Person. Halifax; The Archbishop of Halifax. 1984.

32. Hawkins, Freda. *Canada and Immigration. Public Policy and Public Concern.* Montreal; McGill/Queens University Press. 1972.

33. Honor Young Latvian as 50,000th D.P. Arrival. *The Halifax Chronicle-Herald.* Halifax; 1949; 1(49):22.

34. Hood, John. Unpublished Notes. Halifax; not dated.

35. Inspection Report to Ottawa. Halifax; 1893.

36. JIAS News. Montreal; Jewish Immigrant Aid Society. 1948; 1(8): August 13.

37. JIAS News. Montreal; Jewish Immigrant Aid Society. 1949; February 15.

38. JIAS News. Montreal; Jewish Immigrant Aid Society. 1950; 6(8): December 1.

39. Jewish War Orphans are Entertained at Synagogue. *The Halifax Mail-Star*. Halifax; 1949; 1(29) (January 25) 3.

40. MacKinnon, F.R. British Guest Children — History and Working Papers. Halifax: Unpublished. 1986.

41. MacKinnon, Ian Forbes. *Canada and the Minority Churches of Eastern Europe 1946-1950*. London: Camelot Press Ltd. 1959; 31-37.

42. MacKinnon, U.J. Letter to Mrs. S. Fineberg. Halifax: 1971 January 12.

43. Maylin, Len. Letter to W.C. Boyle. Simcoe; 1979, May 11.

44. Memo to Resident Architect. Dept. of Immigration. Halifax; 1935.

45. Metson, Graham. *An East Coast Port*. Toronto; McGraw-Hill Ryerson Ltd. 1981.

46. Porter, John. *The Vertical Mosaic*. Toronto; University of Toronto Press. 1971.

47. Raddall, Thomas H. *Warden of the North.* Toronto: McClelland and Stewart Ltd. 1971.

48. Raddall, Thomas H. *Hangman's Beach.* Toronto: McClelland and Stewart Ltd. 1979.

49. Report of Commission of Inquiry on Smallpox Outbreak Halifax N.S. Halifax: March 6, 1938; 36-37.

50. Saly, Helene. Letter to W.C. Boyle. Westmount; 1981.

51. Sessional Papers. House of Commons. Ottawa: 1893(7); 56.

52. Sessional Papers. House of Commons. Ottawa: 1867-1920.

53. *The Ensign* 1949: 3, 6.

54. *The Field At Home.* Halifax: The Sisters of Service January 1930: 6-8.

55. *The Halifax Evening-Mail.* Halifax; 1929: October 31.

56. *The Open Gateway.* Halifax Harbour Commissioners. 1932; 1(2) 12.

57. *The Pier 21 Story.* Canada Employment and Immigration Commission. Halifax; 1978.

58. The Women of Halifax. *Chatelaine.* Toronto: 1954; June: 13-17, 104.

59. Tired Baltic Refugees Reach Halifax After Month Long Ocean Trip. Halifax: *The Halifax Chronicle-Herald* 1949; August 20. 58.

60. Tripp, Eleanor B. *To America — The Story of Why People Left Their Homes for a New Land.* New York: Harcourt, Brace & World Inc. 1969.

61. Welcome Doukhobors! To Canada's Free Soil. The *Halifax Herald.* Halifax: 1899; XXV (19)1.

62. *Welcome to War Brides.* The Department of National Defence and The Wartime Information Board. Ottawa: 1944; 18-22.

63. Wolff, Louise S. A Refugee. *The Atlantic Breeze.* Department of Manpower and Immigration. 1972; 6.

64. 1000 War Orphan. *The Halifax Mail-Star.* Halifax: 1949; 1(19) Jaunaru 24. p. 1.

65. 216 War Refugees Reach N.S. *The Halifax Chronicle.* Halifax: 1939; 95 (220) September 14. p. 1.

The Authors

Trudy Duivenvoorden Mitic   **J.P. LeBlanc**

Trudy Duivenvoorden Mitic is the daughter of Dutch immigrants who came to Canada through Pier 21 in the early 1950s. Earlier this year she successfully chronicled her parents' early years in Canada in her first book, ***Canadian By Choice.*** That warm-hearted book details the loneliness and bewilderment that so many immigrants experienced when they first came to this new country, and how they survived and flourished, due to their own strength of character.

Trudy Duivenvoorden Mitic received her BA from Concordia University in Montreal, and her MPE in Recreation from the University of New Brunswick. She and her husband Wayne have two young children.

J.P. LeBlanc is a ninth generation Canadian, and a native of St. Anselme (Dieppe), N.B. He retired in 1982 as Director-General for Nova Scotia with Employment and Immigration Canada. His career as a public servant placed him in Moncton, Ottawa, Vancouver and in Windsor, Ontario, where he was made an honorary citizen in recognition of his generous volunteer efforts.

Mr. LeBlanc is a WW II RCAF veteran with Bomber Command. He headed overseas in 1942 from Pier 21, aboard the **Queen Elizabeth**. His wife is a war bride. He is now Board Director for Nova Scotia with the Canadian Immigration Historical Society.